"*The Lucky One* is a disturbing abuse, human trafficking, evil, and redemption. Too often these stories are hidden or denied. Jenni is a wise, tender, and honest chronicler of a story we'd rather pretend doesn't exist. It does and it is not uncommon. Her story cries out that God does meet us in valley of the shadow of death to invite us face to face to his tender and fierce love. Your heart will be sensitized to a great evil, but far more you too will be invited to taste the goodness of God in the land of the living."

– Dan B. Allender, Ph.D.; Professor of Counseling Psychology, Founding President; The Seattle School of Theology and Psychology

"This book is heartbreaking. Not in the pain that it describes –which is horrific – but in the beauty that it calls out to in the midst of the pain. It is story of courage that helped a young girl survive years of sexual exploitation, and a testimony of a radical love that is available to us all. It is also a challenge for us, the reader, to be vulnerable and courageous in our own lives, just as she was in hers."

– Christa Foster Crawford, Anti-Trafficking Consultant, Trafficking Resource Connection, Adjunct Assistant Professor of Children at Risk, Fuller Theological Seminary, School of Intercultural Studies

"Jenni masterfully weaves steadfast truths into a story that shakes our worldview, our theology and our ideas of what a human can bear. The hope and redemption she found in th e darkest places become available to all of us. We, too, lose our fears as we walk alongside a broken child into wholeness and restored womanhood."

– Hettie Brittz, motivational speaker and author, *Fearless. Free.* and *(un)Natural Mom*

"A Kiswahili saying comes to mind when I think of Jenni's story. "Mungu tu," meaning, "Only God." Only God could bring forth something of profound beauty from Jenni's story. Her life is a testament to God's redemptive power and his healing love. Whether you read this book to try to understand some of the darkness of sex trafficking, or to find healing for your own wounds, you will not be disappointed. May you, too, step back and say, "Mungu tu! Only God..."

– Adele Booysen, D.Min.

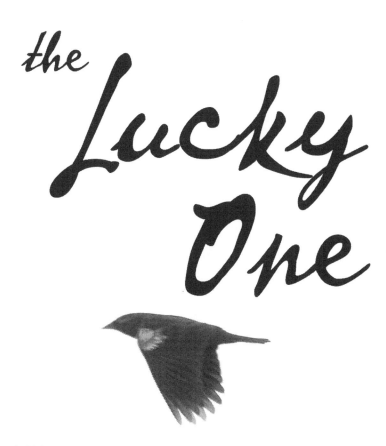

the Lucky One

A chilling true account of child sex trafficking and one survivor's
journey from brutal captivity to a life of freedom.

Jenni S. Jessen

www.compass31.org

The Lucky One

To contact the author and/or request bulk quantities of *The Lucky One*, please email: theluckyone@compass31.org

Unless otherwise noted, all scriptures are taken from the Holy Bible, New International Version. © 1973, 1978, 1984, International Bible Society.

ISBN: 978-0-692-68060-5
Library of Congress Control Number: 2016939070

"Red-winged Blackbird" image courtesy of Dede Lusk
Cover photo of Jenni Jessen by Jason DeFord

Publishing, composition, and design managed by Niche Pressworks
www.nichepressworks.com

Proceeds from the sale of this book go to fight human trafficking.
www.compass31.org

Dedication

To KJ, the love of my life.

The first night we met I knew that you would be my husband but I didn't know your open arms and noble heart would also bring me healing and freedom.

Thank you for all of the nights that you have slept with the lights on because my dark was too near. Thank you for holding me tight through the nightmares that still chase me through the night. Thank you for keeping a safe distance when I can't bear to be touched because the ghosts of my past are still lingering.

My Love, My Prince, thank you for showing me God's faithfulness. It was your broken reflections of His perfect love and your unwavering faith in His goodness that taught me about the trustworthiness of God. I love you.

All ways and Always.

J

Table of Contents

Foreword

N ot many survivors of abuse identify themselves as "the lucky
one." Nor do many survivors meet Jesus for the first time after
being raped. Such is the uniqueness of this book. Jenni's story is an
account of horrifying evil, pain, and hope. It is difficult for most
people to believe that the horrendous events Jenni describes could
really happen. Yet they do. Followers of Jesus have every reason to
believe that evil is real and abuse does happen in frighteningly de-
structive ways. Scripture calls Satan the malevolent "god of this
world" (2 Corinthians 4:4) who has stimulated abuse from the dawn
of human history and will perpetuate it until Jesus returns (1 John
3:12; Revelation 9:11). Scripture gives literally hundreds of descrip-
tions of physical and sexual abuse, often with much more graphic
detail than Jenni's account of her childhood trauma. Consider for
instance, the stories of a fatal gang rape in Judges 19, the incest rape
of Tamar recorded in 2 Samuel 13, and the slaughter, torture, and
assaults described in the book of Lamentations. No one in their right
mind enjoys thinking about such gruesome realities. However, we
must face abuse in order to address it.

No one knows precisely how many children and youth are commercially sexually exploited in the U.S. but experts estimate that as many as 400,000 minors are being or are at the highest risk of being sex trafficked each year. Globally the problem is much greater — even epidemic in some communities. But this book is not just for those concerned about sex trafficking. The latest research indicates that one out of four girls and one out of seven boys will be sexually abused before they reach their eighteenth year. And sadly, college age women appear to be at an even greater risk of sexual abuse. In short, child sexual abuse is an enormous problem that touches a great percentage of our population.

Thankfully, Jenni not only gives us important insights into incest, commercial sexual exploitation and evil, but most importantly, she offers a healing framework. Much like the great fourth and fifth century church father Augustine, Jenni shows how even in the darkest, most painful moments of her past, Jesus was present working on her behalf. Jenni's understanding of "lucky" is not good fortune based on blind chance but rather blessing based on the loving pursuit of her by the God of the universe. Oh that every survivor of abuse would absorb this truth to the marrow of his or her bones — *I'm the lucky one because God has chosen me as His child* — He loves me, no matter what I've done or experienced.

God does not abandon His children; He has not abandoned you. As you read these pages pause and allow the truth of God's love for you to seep in. May you see yourself reflected in His eyes — may His adoring love for you give you courage enough to tell the truth of your story, knowing that you were made for some great end; that there is no earthly evil that can pervert your created, original design. Know that abuse cannot touch your divine essence. You have a unique destiny to fulfill so draw courage from these pages as Jenni takes your hand and steps with you onto a redemptive path.

You never go away from us,
yet we have difficulty in returning to You.
Come, Lord, stir us up and call us back.
Kindle and seize us. Be our fire and our sweetness.
Let us love. Let us run.

—*Augustine of Hippo, Confessions*

Steven R. Tracy, PhD
Professor of Theology and Ethics, Phoenix Seminary
Co-founder & President, Mending the Soul Ministries

Celestia G. Tracy, MA
Co-founder & Director of Resource Development, Mending the Soul
Ministries

CHAPTER 1

Chosen

I was only four years old the first time I met God. It happened just after the rape. It was a hot summer day and I went with my grandfather to the train station. He worked for FRISCO and had arranged for me to ride with a conductor on the engine of a train. The excitement was palpable as the noise of the chugging train rattled through my petite body. I spent much of the day traveling in the engine through the train yard moving railcars back and forth like a giant sliding number puzzle. I delighted in blowing a whistle that rang clear down deep in my bones. My sandy blonde pigtails bounced as I explored the maze of powerful boxes lined up orderly in iron tracks. The rattling sights and sounds both stirred and fed my insatiable curiosity. The day was crammed with about as much adventure as a green eyed girl-child could bear. I was filled with pleasant exhaustion by the time the last cars were put into their proper places. My grandfather and the conductor began walking over the tracks and through the cars out into a nearby field. Though my feet had grown weary, I skipped behind them willingly, happily. The field of golden grass was nearly as tall as I was. Crickets and grasshoppers shouted greetings as we tromped carelessly through their territory. Shortly, we arrived at my grandfather's car parked in the middle of the empty field. It surprised and confused me to see his brand new Lincoln Mark IV sitting there when I could see nothing else but a huge blue sky and the waving grass. My grandfather turned to me with a smile that suddenly caused my blood to curdle cold despite the heat of the day. He opened the trunk of the car and pulled out some long strips of fabric and walked towards me. An unspeakable darkness clouded his eyes. Panic rose and fastened my tiny feet to the ground where I stood.

"Did you have fun playing at the train station today?" he asked.

"Yes, Papa. I loved making the whistle blow." I answered warily.

"Well, now we are going to play another game, okay? You put your hands out here for me and I'll tell you how to play."

The laughter in his black eyes haunted me, but at four years old the only thing I was really an expert at was play. I put out my hands for him and watched as he bound them together. The binding was not uncomfortable, it was loose enough to not leave a mark, but just tight enough to prevent my escape.

In the moments that followed, my grandfather completed his business transaction with the engineer and walked a few yards away. Then the engineer took from me what he had paid for. That summer day in 1976 was the first time that I was sold for sex. This was the first time that I was taken by force; the first time someone other than my grandfather used me to satisfy his lust, but this was not the first time I had had sex. My virginity had already been stolen by my grandfather some time long before this event; long before my memory could keep an accurate account.

6

The trauma of that afternoon tore a hole clear through my spirit and opened up for me the realm in which soul and body can be divided into two. While my body was brutalized, my heart flew into the scarlet and ginger hues of a sunset on fire. My screams were carried away with the falling sun. It was there that Jesus came for me.

When the violence subsided, my grandfather returned and wrapped me up in an old army blanket. His rough hands suddenly gentle, he set me tenderly on a towel in the backseat of the car to take me home. He slid into the driver's seat and then while he mumbled something about what a good girl I was, he perpetrated his most heinous act of the day. He started a cassette tape playing, "How Great Thou Art." His brutal need for control and his cruel sense of humor collided in a love for old gospel music. As such he would often play that particular song over and over either during or immediately following the torture that I was repeatedly subjected to. My grandfather intended to keep me bound in captivity for life and "How Great Thou Art" provided him the chains he would use to accomplish his purposes. His choice in music was a deliberate attempt to ensure that I would never... NO... not ever find comfort in a church or freedom in Christ.

For many years this tactic was highly effective. The reaction I had to the song would cause tears silenced for years to leap forth declaring the untold story. My body would tremble and stomach revolt. I would have to leave the church and be unable to return for the rest of the service. Even now, I have a strong reaction to the song when it creeps into a worship service. Though I no longer need to flee when I hear it, still the refrain kicks me in the gut and leaves me gasping for breath. My grandfather's strategy might have worked forever, but for the grace of the One who promises to never leave or forsake us.

The road home was long that evening. The golden wheat fields stood sentinel nodding their heads in acknowledgement of my grief.

Serenaded by a gospel singer I watched the sun disappearing in a riot of colors. The singer crooned about a "power throughout the universe displayed," and I couldn't begin to grasp a power greater than that held by my grandfather. I did not fear the approaching darkness as the sun fled because the dark had already come crashing into my world. It was beyond my imagining that night could bring terrors worse than those I had just endured. Waves of nausea wrestled with the melody of the song playing over and over again on the radio.

And then Jesus wrapped His arms around me. He held me tightly in the backseat. He did not mind my blood on His lap or my tears silently raining down on His scarred hands. Jesus leaned close to my ear, breath hot on my fragile neck and with fierce determination He whispered,

"I've gotcha, baby. You are mine. I AM big enough for this. No matter what happens, I AM not going to let you go."

I wonder what my grandfather would have seen, had he looked back in his rearview mirror. Would the eyes of the Savior who held me tightly have struck him with terror? I don't know. I do know that the Jesus that I experienced that day when I was four years old was every bit as real as my grandfather, or the engineer, or the wheat, or the sunset.

It is nearly impossible for a mature mind to grasp the sovereignty of God, let alone a child whose world has been wrecked by the savage lust of men. But with God all things are possible. Ephesians 1:4 says,

"For He chose us in Him before the creation of the world to be holy and blameless in His sight. In love, He predestined us to be adopted..."

It would be another sunset some 24 years later that God would use with that verse to begin unraveling the promises He had spoken to me that summer afternoon so long before.

It happened on a cool Colorado evening while the sun was laying His glory down behind the mountains that guarded our valley. The sky was filled with familiar strokes of crimson and orange and without warning Ephesians 1:4 leapt off the page and sprang to life in the rocky soil of my heart. In that moment everything that I knew and everything that I had experienced began to shift. The tectonic plates of trauma and sovereignty, slammed into one another and the subsequent shock waves left me unsteady for days. It is indeed true that when the Word becomes flesh in the here and now it changes us.

As Ephesians 1:4 sank deep into my desert-parched bones, I asked myself if it might not be possible that God chose not only us collectively as the verse suggests, but that He chooses us individually, personally. Being chosen was significant for me. I knew what it was to be chosen. Again and again, I had been chosen and devoured by those who feed on fear and blood. But to be chosen by the Creator God held altogether different implications.

Could it be that I was chosen by God in a way that meant safety instead of danger; that I was selected by Jesus in a way that meant freedom instead of captivity; that He preferred me in a way that meant healing instead of wounding? Could this be possible even when memories came in nightmares and chased me relentlessly through dark nights and when physical scars still screamed of the damage done? I couldn't immediately grasp the magnitude of what Truth was confronting my realities, but I spun dizzy in the possibilities.

The lessons for my heart continued. The word in Ephesians suggests that not only did He choose us, but that He did so at a specific time. "Before the creation of the world," the Word says. That means that from infinite time past God looked throughout the ages. He looked and He saw you. He looked and He saw me. In that time before all-time began, He declared, "That one, Jenni, she is mine. She is holy. She is blameless. In love I will adopt her as my own..."

When the Spirit hovered over the dark, empty void that would come to be our world; before He flipped on the lights of this universe with a word; before God drew a line between the sky above and the waters below, He called you. He called me. He called us His own. He called us collectively. He called us personally.

God chose us at a specific time and He chose us for a specific purpose. Jesus, knowing full well the depth of the trauma that I would endure as a child, the profound shame I would learn to carry, the mistrust that I would harbor about who He is, knowing all of this and more, God chose to call me holy. He chose to call me blameless. He chose to adopt me as His own. What kind of crazy grace is that?

God saw the countless times that I would submit instead of fight. He saw that by the time I finished kindergarten I would be as proficient at seduction as I was at my ABCs. He saw that I would willingly trade whatever favors were necessary to survive the grip of the next man that claimed me. Not only would I bear the disgrace of the many ways my body was broken and used and bear the humiliation of how I learned to survive by bargaining with my captors, but I would later run as far and as fast as my legs could carry me from the only Man who could ever teach me what real love is; Jesus. I would rebel. I would despise and reject Him. I would rage and wail against Him. I would call Him weak and vehemently lay out my case against His goodness and grace.

Crazy grace is Jesus seeing all of that. It is Him seeing all of our guilt and all of our shame and yet choosing us anyway. He chooses to call us holy. He chooses to call us blameless. He chooses us as His own.

When I began to comprehend the truths of this verse and how they fulfilled the promises I heard whispered breathy and wild so long before, I began to find healing. I began to see how His hand had protected me through the years. I began to understand the many ways that Jesus had intervened on my behalf. Though my body was ravaged time after time, my spirit had always been able to fly away until the worst was over. My body was held captive through the years, but my spirit was never once caged. That is crazy grace.

The other thing that is crazy about grace is that it is not meant for me alone. It is for each of us, for all of us. I am not the exception to the rule, nor are you. Before you put this down and rush on to the million things demanding your attention, I invite you to experience the One who chose you by name before the creation of the world.

Read Ephesians 1:4 again. Take a deep breath and close your eyes. Wait for Him. Listen for His still, small voice pushing open the doors of your heart. Jesus is calling you His own. He is calling you holy and blameless. He is calling you loved. Can you hear Him whispering "My chosen one"? Can you hear in the wind or the rain His song of love over you? You might hear it with your ears. You might hear it with your gut. You might hear it with images flashing through your memory like old black and white family films.

There are as many ways to hear His voice as there are ears to hear it. None of us hear Him the same. He speaks through His Word. I invite you, open a Bible, open your heart. If you ask Him, He will speak. Bask in His presence for a moment, then a moment more. Stay here long as you like. Jesus is in no hurry. Rest in His love for you. Listen to what Truth He whispers over you, and let it change you.

CHAPTER 2

Dark Roads

The first time I remember being abused happened within the week that I turned three. Strange isn't it? Many people cannot remember anything that happened before the age of 10. I have often wished I was one of those. My life would be different, I think, but so would my faith.

Wrapped in miles of yellow ruffles, I sat perched on my knees in the middle of the front seat of my grandfather's car. The curves of the road slithered in the gleam of the headlights. Trees loomed on either side of the road like spectators in a coliseum. The light of the dashboard barely illuminated the features of this man whom I loved. His dark hair was lost in the shadows and the unnatural blue glow caused his chin and cheeks to look sharp. He fiddled with the radio a bit and when he could not find music to suit his mood, he turned his attention on me.

First, his rough calloused hand rested casually on my knee. It did not startle or surprise me; I was quite used to his familiar touch. But this night, Grandfather's knowing smile stirred a treacherous feeling deep within me. His hand slid slowly between my legs. I did not know enough yet to resist the attention and affection of my grandfather. The seduction was masterful. As I responded to his touch he probed deeper until he reached that place inside of me where fear dwelt. My body trembled and ached and nausea unfolded in my stomach as I watched the road spread out before us.

Suddenly as we came up over a hill the headlights of the car shone on a man who stood directly in our path. In a moment that seemed to last an eternity I watched the brutal scene unfold. The man, crossing the road, turned to look at his approaching end and froze mid-stride. In a vain attempt to shield himself, he threw his arms up over his curly black head. I watched in slow motion as the bundle of blue flannel and denim collided with the front of the car and then flipped up over the windshield.

The sound of my grandfather's cursing mixed in a deadly melody with the violent blow of death. The car careened to the side and stopped with a loud screech of rebellion. My grandfather turned to me as a ghastly calm slid into the dark car.

"You will sit still and you will not turn around. Do you understand me?"

Unable to speak or even breathe, I did not respond. He clutched my arms tightly and with a shake repeated his instruction.

"DO YOU UNDERSTAND?"

Fear spoke for me, "Yes, Papa." I mumbled without the least understanding of what had just happened.

My grandfather got out of the car. The momentary glare of the inside light was a blinding shock to the darkness that covered us. The door slammed, and he walked behind the car, still muttering curses under his breath. I was obedient and stayed rooted firmly in my seat, but from my vantage point, I watched in the rear view mirror as the grisly crime scene was concealed.

In the pale white glow of the rear lights of the car, my grandfather crouched down over the crumpled victim on the side of the road. He rummaged through the bloody pockets and pulled something free. He stalked back to the car and tossed a brown wallet into the back floorboard. Reaching down into the back seat he retrieved a dirty rag. Shoving the rag into his back pocket he returned to the body. Glancing down the road and over his shoulder, my grandfather stooped to put his hands under arms of the rumpled body on the road. As he lifted the man's shoulders and began to drag him off into the night, the man's head rolled forward. His vacant eyes were wide with disbelief and his face frozen in a moment of shock and pain. A crimson stream flowed from his mouth and nose. I choked and gasped as I looked death full in the face.

My grandfather and the man disappeared into the brush on the side of the road, and I tried hard to remember how to breathe in the emptiness. Out of the darkness, my grandfather stepped back into the light. Wiping his bloody hands on the rag he carried, he approached the car. Getting in, he turned to me and explained to me what my three-year-old mind could not grasp.

"Now, Jennifer, I want you to listen closely. Are you listening to Papa? What happened is very, very bad. That man who we hit with the car, he died. Do you understand? We killed that man. It is not okay to kill someone, and if we tell anyone at all, then I am afraid the police will have to take you to jail. When little girls go to jail, they don't have mommies and daddies anymore. Do you understand? You can't kill somebody and get away with it."

Wrapping his huge arms around my shrinking frame, he whispered softly as he masterfully wove the deceptions. "Now I promise

I won't tell anyone, okay? I don't want such a sweet little girl like you to go to jail. After all, you didn't mean to kill the man, did you? I know you didn't mean it, but the police, well, they wouldn't understand. Okay?"

My head nodded yes more out of weakness than commitment, but all the same, we were in agreement. I would not tell and neither would he. My grandfather pulled the car back onto the road and drove the remaining couple of miles to my home in silence. As we pulled into the drive, he explained the game we were going to play.

"Do you know how to pretend, Jennifer? We are going to pretend that you are asleep. I will carry you in to your bed and when you wake up in the morning, this will be all a dream."

My grandfather picked me up and I settled against his Old-Spice scented chest with my eyes tightly closed. He carried me inside and as I pretended to sleep, I listened to the alcohol slurred acknowledgement of my parents.

Raggedy Ann and a stuffed monkey named ChiChi were the only witnesses to my grandfather's whispered words as he tucked me in that night. It was both a promise and a warning.

"Remember Jennifer, this is all a bad dream."

That night I lay awake for a long time trying to figure out what the difference between being asleep and being awake was. As I lay there I listened to my grandfather weave a tale of shock and humor.

"Yeah, just right out in front of me... I came up over the hill, and the deer was standing right there in the middle of the road. I tried to swerve but those damned animals, they get caught in the headlights and nothing can move them. Well, nothing but the grill of the car...Yeah, I think it shook up Jennifer a little bit. There was fur flying...Yeah, it put a pretty good dent in the front of the car....quite a bit of blood....I'll clean it up in the morning before I run over to the insurance office...damn deer!"

A deer... a deer... my grandfather was protecting me. After all, you can't get away with killing a man.

Dark country roads still haunt me in a way I have never yet been able to escape. Perhaps it is rooted in this one memory, but more than likely, it is because of the many other clandestine meetings that took place on such menacing backwoods roads. Even now, should I find myself driving without my husband on some moonlight road overshadowed with trees, panic is my constant companion. I have tried to outrun him, tried to throw him from the car, yet he stifles and suffocates me with his steely grip.

I wonder, do my children know this? Are they ever aware of the threatening passenger that only shows himself in the blue glow of the dashboard lights? I pray that they have not met this one named Panic who still chases me. I pray that they never will.

We want to believe that healing means that we will no longer experience pain from past wounds. We want it to mean that there are no more nightmares; that a life devastated can be made over in such a way as to erase what has gone before. When we give ourselves over to faith, especially faith in Jesus, we may soon become disillusioned when the nightmares recur and the scars linger. The enemy whispers that God is weak or that He doesn't care. We are tempted to believe it. However, it is our belief that is wrong-not His power nor His love.

When I was 9 years old, I fell on a playground during a careless moment of play. My clumsiness resulted in 4 stitches in my lower lip. The scar remains to this day. If I live to be 99 the scar will still mark the place where my teeth bit through tender flesh. The wound does not bleed any more. The purple swelling faded away and new skin grew covering the gash. Yet the scar remains. It always will.

Newton's third law of physics tells us that for every action, there is an equal and opposite reaction. There are always consequences to sin. Experiencing healing doesn't mean our scars disappear. The impact remains long after the blood ceases to flow and the pain subsides. At the time of this writing, I have been free from my grandfather for more than half of my life. Even still, I sometimes wake my husband in the middle of the night flying into the shelter of his arms as I flee the terror of my past. My freedom is complete, but my scars remain.

The scars that we bear testify of the One God who is sovereign even in the darkness. My heart holds so many stories of brutality and survival, most of which, I simply am not strong enough to write down. Instead those memories are carved deeply into the sinews of my soul and my flesh. Those very scars proclaim God's glory even when my trembling voice is too weak to do so.

What scars do you have that testify of God's intervention on your behalf?

CHAPTER 3

Little Boy Blue

With bare feet, I slipped away from chaos. Stealing down the long hallway that separated our living quarters from the operational side of a funeral home, I rushed breathlessly toward rest. The door, closed but never locked, opened into a world of perfect stillness. In this place, quietness prevailed.

At 5 years old I had found a place of refuge, it was my shalom. The funeral home was a honeycomb of spaces from which I gleaned critical survival skills. The cavernous halls were lined with chameleon-like side rooms that could be transformed with the wave of a hand. In a moment, those rooms could change from a family room to a sanctuary to a hiding place for the bereaved. Within them I learned to blend, to camouflage, to appear however necessary to accommodate the demands of the moment.

The casket room, stacked with tiers of beautiful human-sized treasure chests, taught me all about the impenetrable, outward shell of beauty that stands guard over gaping emptiness. The embalming room, clothed only with stainless steel and white tile, stood silent and sterile. It taught me about the cold metal detachment of secret keeping. Juxtaposed only a few steps away, the stain-glassed chapel held the heart-wrenching cries of those left behind in fragments of shattered glass. It proclaimed with courage my own savage grief.

Perhaps I should be, but I was never bothered by death. It seemed such a beautiful reprieve. I would go there often, sometimes daily, alone, in search of those whom I believed were the lucky ones. Approaching the chapel silently, I watched the light filtering colored through images of Christendom memorialized in glass, the shattered colors melding together into a cohesive picture imprinted on my soul.

I came boldly to the centerpieces of this room; the yawning coffins waiting to be filled with final goodbyes. I pulled up a small wooden kneeling bench to increase my stature, and I stood with the dead unwavering and unafraid. I would study the marbled lines and veins of men's hands: once strong, now cool. I would look at the old women and wonder how old you had to get for your hair to turn Easter egg blue. But those who really drew me, the ones who invited me to rest, were the little ones.

It was a tiny, flaxen haired boy in the summer of '77 that changed my life. I imagined that his eyes would have matched the light blue of his crisply pressed sailor suit, were he able to open them and look around. Tucked gently in his left hand was the pacifier that had been tied to a cord around his neck on the Wednesday afternoon that he didn't wake up from his nap. On that fateful day, his small comfort had become a noose that carried him into eternity. He had only lived for 18 months, while I had already survived 5 and a half years of the unthinkable.

I put my hand to my throat and squeezed slowly. I held my breath and wondered how long I would have to hold it before I could cross the bridge into the land of the quiet. Seconds ticked by as my lungs rebelled against my determination. Finally, unwillingly, I gasped for breath and sat down and wept. I was jealous of the little boy in blue.

It is the first prayer I ever remember uttering, but one that I would repeat every night for many years to come. "God, please, PLEASE don't make me wake up in the morning."

Trapped in a little girl body, in an upside-down world, I couldn't fathom the concept of suicide. But what I found in that baby boy's casket was a peace that surpassed understanding. So, with child-like faith, I pled daily for mercy, for escape.

"God, please just take me to heaven. I promise I will be a good girl. Just don't make me wake up again."

Much to my angry bewilderment, it was a request that He would adamantly refuse again and again. More than 30 years have passed since that first anguished plea, and still God makes the sun come up each morning. Still, He puts breath within my chest and causes my heart, broken a thousand times over, to drum on. It has been many years since I last prayed for death to steal me away. But still, in the trauma of life in a fallen world, an echo remains deep within me. Calling gently, ever whispering, someday, there will be rest. Some-day, there will be peace. Someday, there will be justice. Someday, someday, this all will end well.

Many people view death as an enemy, something to be feared or conquered at all cost. Perhaps that is because they have a limited view. We who have lived in the hazy realm of the in-between, know differently. Those of us who have learned to straddle the fence be-tween death and life view things through an altered lens. We know that every good thing we have ever experienced here on earth is only a dim and dirty shadow of what awaits us with God in eternity.

The phrase "near death experience" is only accurately applied to those who do not know Jesus. For those who are Christ followers, it is a tragic misunderstanding. Truly, they are "near life experiences."

As a child I prayed again and again for Jesus to take me away. In truth, He did. He took me away from my broken body chained captive. While my flesh endured violence incomprehensible, my spirit danced in the light of His presence. What angered me most was not that He refused to take me, but that He always made me come back. When I prayed desperately for the rescue born of death, He forced me to live. I can relate to the demon possessed man in Mark 5:1-17. The man called himself, "Legion" because that is how many demons tormented and held him captive. After he was set free from bondage, the man begged to go with Jesus.

"But Jesus did not let him, but said,
"Go home to your family and tell them how much
the Lord has done for you,
and how He has had mercy on you."

Mark 6:19

So did I. I came back and continue even still to proclaim His mercy, but this is no simple cliché. There are no easy answers to the why and how of His intervention into my life or others.

Many times over the years, I have overheard well-meaning friends tell others that "God won't give you more than you can bear." When I hear those beautiful but false words, my heart bangs against my chest raging at the suggestion. It is adding insult to injury to offer someone with terminal grief a Band-Aid platitude. God does, in fact, give us more than we can bear. He does it again and again. It doesn't slander or belittle Him to tell the truth about it. The Truth sets us free. A kindergartener that pleads daily with God for death is carrying more than any child can bear. Someone must carry that for her. Jesus alone can bear the weight that is too great for the human spirit to survive.

There are two important lessons I learned from Little Boy Blue. The first was that death is nothing to be feared. Death is only the doorway that opens for us the most real and most true life. As much as we would like to believe otherwise, no one escapes death. Ten out of ten people will die. We will each look death full in the face and we will each be overcome by it. There will come a time in each of our lives that a person, or an accident, or an act of violence, or a disease will help us take off these scarred cadavers once and for all. When death comes for each of us then no chains will remain. We will be free to dance in His presence forever. No longer bound by skin and weighed down by gravity we will cry out, "O Death, where is your sting?"

The second thing that I learned was that we can become fully aware of Jesus' presence at any given moment. Psalm 139 gives us a glimpse into this truth. David writes,

"Where can I go from your Spirit?
Where can I flee from your presence?
If I go up to the heavens, you are there;
if I make my bed in the depths, you are there.

If I rise on the wings of the dawn,
if I settle on the far side of the sea,
even there your hand will guide me,
your right hand will hold me fast.

If I say, "Surely the darkness will hide me
and the light become night around me,"

even the darkness will not be dark to you;
the night will shine like the day,
for darkness is as light to you."

If the Word of God is true, then these verses pose a startling hypothesis. Is it possible that there is nowhere on heaven or earth that you or I are outside of God's presence? Many times, both as a child and as an adult, I have felt as if my prayers have gone no further than the flat white ceiling above me before fluttering lifelessly to the ground. Perhaps you have felt that way too?

Could it be that Jesus, who was acquainted with sorrows, is raking those prayers like fallen leaves into piles of glorious color? Bright leaves that shout His glory, even as death approaches in cold sunsets and shuttering winds. Not one sparrow, not one hair on our heads, not one child falls without His notice.

He does give us more than we can bear, but Jesus is alive and He never leaves us alone for a minute. My experience has taught me what David knew to be true. There is nowhere that we are outside of His presence. In the depths where oceans of grief threaten to drown us, He is there. In the bright dawn where our shame is exposed, He is there. Jesus sees in the darkness as clearly as He sees in the day.

You too, may have been abandoned by those who should have protected you. Like me, you may have felt abandoned by God. The traumas you have faced may far exceed my own. You may need to summon all of your courage and bare your wounds to the One who bears all of our pain. You may need to do as I did and pour all of your furious questions on Him who is without sin.

I have shouted at Him, "Where were you!?! Why didn't you protect me? Why didn't you just let me die?"

I did not deserve an answer. The Most High God doesn't owe us an explanation…ever. He is God. Period. Yet in the quiet dark Jesus did answer me. A quick succession of memories flashed through my mind; four years old…five…eight…fifteen years old. Traumas ran together like raindrops gliding down glass. Dark places, countless men, savage abuses.

There was only one constant in each image: Jesus. In every memory He was there. He held me. He pulled my spirit away. He hid my eyes from the worst while He didn't look away for a moment. He was fully present and bearing all of the pain and shame that I couldn't possibly carry. Since childhood; I had been angry that God didn't rescue me, but He doesn't promise rescue. God promises to never leave us and never to forsake us.

It is one thing to consider that God is fully present in trauma, but how often do we consider Him fully present in our day-to-day lives? As we pull ourselves from warm blankets and restless sleep; as we scurry out of the house too busy to stop for breakfast; as we rush hither and yon in the bustle of a million insignificant things that must be done, do we ever pause grateful that our heart continues to beat? Do we ever become aware that every single breath comes from the God who created us?

Even now, there may be a thousand things pulling you back into the demands of your day-to-day life. Before you go, won't you take a moment and become aware of God's presence? He is sitting here with me. He is sitting there with you. Talk to Him. If you are angry, tell Him. If you have questions, ask Him. You can't shock the omniscient One. You can't outrun the omnipresent One.

In the here and now, I challenge you to be fully present, to be with Jesus whose name is Emmanuel, God with us.

CHAPTER 4

Broken

A dingy motel room on the side of the road in southern Missouri guards a few of my secrets of brokenness. The neon sign, only partially lit, flashes MOTEL with letters hanging precariously and buzzing loudly. I do not know how much that man paid my grandfather for my time, but he most certainly did not splurge on the room. The bedspread hanging crooked on a double bed must have been stylish somewhere, sometime. But the pattern of avocado and brown printed haphazardly on the polyester-blend fabric could have only been rightly named, "Vomit."

I was well-trained and well-practiced by the ripe old age of 8. I knew well that my survival depended on my submission. I knew how to play the role in which I had been cast. But on that particular day, that particular man did not respond to me as others had. In fact, his body didn't respond at all.

In any other frame of reference, an impotent pedophile would be a good thing. This man, however, with giant hands and dirty overalls held me personally responsible for his performance failure. Perhaps I was not pretty enough. Maybe I was not seductive enough. His rage rose dangerously when nothing else would. He lashed out with a closed-fist-backhand that sent me sprawling backwards, landing dizzily, ragdoll-style in the corner of the tiny room. Black haze crowded the corners of my vision as stars flitted through my consciousness. Fists pounded and feet bludgeoned my body as I huddled tightly in fetal position.

Then the unthinkable happened. Ralph, my grandfather and my primary perpetrator, barged into the room and became my savior. He grabbed the right arm of the raging man, attempting to pull him back. But when his efforts to intervene were easily thwarted, my grandfather put himself in the in-between. Heavy feet and long arms no longer landed on my wilting body but Ralph received the blows in my place. By the time he carried me to the car that afternoon, he had garnered a few bruises of his own while my sacrum had been broken in three places and two cervical vertebrae were fractured.

Many survivors do not know the moment that it happened, the exact moment that they bonded to their perpetrator. Counselors call this unfathomable concept trauma bonding. Trauma bonding is defined as, "strong emotional ties that develop between two persons where one person intermittently harasses, beats, threatens, abuses, or intimidates the other."[1]

Before this event, I knew who the bad guy was but suddenly I was no longer sure. My fear of Ralph turned to awe as he stepped in to protect me. This shift in love and loyalty wrecked my world and further adds to the complexity of escape and ultimately finding healing and restoration.

---

[1] Dutton, D.G and Painter, S.L. (1981) "Traumatic Bonding: the development of emotional attachments in battered women and other relationships of intermittent abuse." Victimology: An International Journal, 1(4), pp. 139–155

That day when I was 8 years old, I came to believe a couple of very significant lies. These lies gave me a new lens through which I would process all further experiences. The first lie was that I deserved whatever happened to me; the second was that Ralph was my protector.

Ralph became my god. In the view from my little green eyes, he alone wielded the power to determine what my body would endure and what punishments or rewards I would receive. He could step in at any time with rough-tender hands as my defending savior. Conversely, with a sinister grin, he could force me into the bed of a sadist. I lived in an insane world that always teetered on the brink of unsure.

Bewildered people often ask me, "Why didn't you tell anyone?" There is no easy answer to that question but it is woven deep in crimson threads of loyalty and love. I loved my grandfather. I wanted desperately what any child wants: to be cherished and to be protected. So I turned all of my attention, my skills and my heart to learning how to be what he expected me to be. But man was never intended to be a god, and Ralph was most certainly unqualified for the job. When any person or thing takes the place of the Most High God, we are on dangerous ground.

I mistakenly placed my faith in a capricious man who took pleasure in pain. But I once heard a startling question in a Bible study. The teacher made a case based on James 1:16-18,

> *"Do not be deceived, my beloved brothers. Every good*
> *gift and every perfect gift is from above, coming down*
> *from the Father of lights with whom there is no*
> *variation or shadow due to change. Of His own will*
> *He brought us forth by the word of truth, that we*
> *should be a kind of firstfruits of His creatures."*

This teacher said that every good thing that ever happened in your life was a gift from God above, even if it came at the hand of an otherwise-abusive person. For years, I had tried to "honor" my grandfather and obey without question, hoping that even if I did not gain his love, I might at least gain a short reprieve from the torment. I had put my faith in him as a good person who just sometimes did bad things. I even came to believe that the bad things he did were the result of my own faults or flaws.

As I listened to the teaching, my struggle to reconcile my loyalty to Ralph with the violence he displayed began wavering dangerously on a precipice. From the outside looking in, any normal person can see a perpetrator for what he is. Unfortunately, things are not so clear when seen through the eyes of a child whose very life depends on the whims of evil.

I mistakenly had given Ralph far too much credit. That summer day when he stepped in, Ralph was not my savior. He was neither my protector, nor was he supposed to be my god. Ralph was not a good person who occasionally meted out just punishments. He was wicked to the core.

Make no mistake about it.

It was Jesus who stepped in that day. The Bible says that every good and perfect gift comes from God. Jesus intervenes to guard and protect. But let's be honest: the manner in which God steps in is often not the way in which we would hope. It was not beneath Jesus, nor does it alter His holiness for Him to show up in a cheap, Midwestern motel room. Jesus moved in; and in His wake a depraved man was compelled to act. Ralph did not step into the in-between and take the blows I deserved. The wounds he received were only tiny glimmers of justice falling on the rightful party. Those who exploit the vulnerable may reign powerfully for a while, but they will not reign forever. My own sin was that I mistakenly gave Ralph my allegiance. But let me cry out with the ancients. Please dear one, hear this if nothing else,

"The Lord our God, the Lord is one. You shall love the Lord your God with all your heart and with all your soul and with all your might. And these words that I command you today shall be on your heart. You shall teach them diligently to your children, and shall talk of them when you sit in your house, and when you walk by the way, and when you lie down, and when you rise."

Deuteronomy 6:4-7

God alone is our Savior. He alone is our Protector. He alone is God. He is the God of Justice whose name is Jealous. There is no other. Take a moment to consider in what or whom you have placed your faith. Is it possible for you to believe that every good thing that has ever happened in your life was orchestrated by God's grace and His love for you?

CHAPTER 5

Girl from Oz

If only the ruby slippers worked in reverse, I would have used the magical shoes to click my way out of the Midwest and into the Land of Oz. Every year, as I watched on a rabbit-eared television how Dorothy would make her journey through the tornado, into Oz and back again, I wondered, 'Why does she go back?'

I only understood the wild, slashing winds of the tornado, the dark of the storm, the gray of an existence devoid of safety or joy. My house was in the perpetual state of spinning out of control. How I longed to crash into a world of color and wonder! I lived vicariously on the yellow brick road, longing for the tender friendship of Scarecrow, the affectionate loyalty of the Tin Man and most of all the protection of that cowardly Lion. The wicked witch held no power of terror over me; she was so small in comparison to my villains. The flying monkeys, swooping and screeching, only seemed to me a means of escape. They were certainly less fearsome than the men I faced in the dark of night. When my door would creak open in wee dark hours and I would be awakened to soul invading darkness, I would look to the window. Where is my Lion, my Tin Man, where is my Scarecrow? If it were only possible for a chattering monkey to fly down and carry me off to the castle, I would gladly face a furious witch rather than the unbridled lust of a beast dressed as a man! If only I could trade a bloody nightgown for garnet shod feet I would click myself to Oz and never, ever come back.

It has been said that the stories that move us do so because they in some part mirror the fables of our own lives and our own hearts. It is certainly true of me and The Wizard of Oz. I longed to be Dorothy. I sought answers and searched hungrily for safety; looking for shelter on dusty Midwestern roads all the while yearning for a yellow brick road somewhere on the other side of the rainbow.

There are many places that we are taught to find safety. Police officers and pastors are supposed to be men who selflessly protect the vulnerable. The vast majority of men who give their lives to serve their communities either in law enforcement or in ministry are good men. Even more so, they are often mighty men, living their lives sacrificially so that others can know freedom, physically and spiritually. If it were always true, I think we would see the kingdom of heaven breaking into our world more often. But, it is not always so, is it? Sometimes the men who should be our protectors instead become our captors. It is a dangerous reality when protectors turn into predators.

As a child I knew a police officer who let me flip the switch that made the siren shriek and lights on his police car flash red and blue. He often allowed me to delight in playing before he delighted in my pain. As easily as unbuttoning his uniform shirt he switched from civic guardian into the monster whom all children fear hides under their beds. In the moments that followed, I wished that I had the same freedom as the siren to cry out. I longed to break the curse of darkness with my screams, but I was betrayed by my voice as well as by Ralph. When I opened my mouth to scream, breathless fear escaped in place of any sound. Throughout years of brutality, depths of trauma, in all that I have experienced, truly there is nothing more terrifying than a scream that has no voice.

On a warm Sunday morning later that same summer, I sat in a church beside my grandfather. My emerald eyes boring into the back of the head of the man who had paid to rape me the night before. With feet swinging from a wooden pew I gawked at combed down stripes of greasy black hair. His ears protruded awkwardly from a head much too small to carry them. His left arm draped loosely around the shoulders of a graying, timid wife who looked more like a mouse playing dress up than a woman. Though I tried earnestly to focus my attention on God that morning, I could not escape the images or lingering pain from the brutality of the night before. Then it happened. Church over, we stood to leave. The man turned around and looking me straight in the eye, shook hands with Ralph. His wife reached out to touch my cheek.

"Such a pretty little thing, isn't she?" Her words fluttered softly to the ground and scurried away quiet.

I walked as if dead, my body moving forward without my spirit, toward the light of the open doorway while I absorbed the trifling Sunday morning chatter. This man was accepted and I was bewildered. He was liked, as was my grandfather. With heads held high they made their way to the door. Without hesitation or shame they stopped to chat with the preacher; just good ole boys shaking hands, talking jovially, a slap on the back, a 'see you next week.'

That particular preacher was not one of my perpetrators, although another one in a different time and place was. Still, on that Sunday morning, he shook hands with the dark. He stood smiling with the perpetrators. Any semblance of potential protection a church might offer seemed paltry at best. Rather than being a place of reprieve, the church became for me a stained glass venue showcasing darkness. If there was hope to be found, that summer taught me that it would not be found in a church, a pastor or a police officer. My grandfather had friends everywhere and I had no one. And so I longed for Oz.

I believe that our innate connection to story poses two stunning evidences for the veracity of a creator God. The first evidence is observed in our souls' intrinsic bond to the great stories. The legends written between 'once upon a times' and 'happily ever afters' inexplicably draw us. We write ourselves into the storylines of those epic narratives and choose roles for ourselves: sometimes the villain, sometimes the hero. Waiting desperately for rescue or sweeping in with golden sword slashing, we enter into the great dramas. This is why leather-bound classics still sell in an age of technology. It is why a two-hour movie can make millions and millions of dollars. Somewhere in the fiber of our soul, we know we are part of an epic story.

With a word God spoke the world into existence. Words move us still.

The second evidence is that a child held captive will still continue to dream. Why? If suffering and trauma are all that exists for her; if there is no point to our existence; if we are just evolutionary accidents spinning from nothingness and into nothingness, then why? Why does she, why did I, dream of more?

I believe that we dream of freedom because we are made in the image of the creator God. Once upon a time, humanity was carved out of the dirt and sprang to life with His life-breath. Our heart pounds out the rhythm of life. "ETERNITY" is engraved into the messy red clay of our flesh. A hope and a future are embedded deeply into the sinews and tendons of humanity. Even a child who has known nothing but sorrow and depravation longs for something more. When I slept, I dreamt freedom. Even in the nightmares that haunt me to this day, I am always running. Gasping and panic-driven I am running away from the dark, and I am running toward safety. I am always running toward freedom, running toward the happily ever after. This is proof of life. I believe it is also proof of God.

What story moves you? Look back on your life up to this point as if watching a movie for the first time. How does your own journey parallel the dramas of your favorite stories? Where did your once upon a time begin and have you found your happily ever after? Spend a few minutes asking God what His role in your story has been. You are part of a bigger narrative; your role is both important and strategic. You are not an extra, but a main character in an epic that will echo throughout time. Ask Him what happily ever after looks like in the messy mundane of ordinary life. Listen to His plot unfold.

CHAPTER 6

A Rebel Soul

It caught me off guard the other day to be laid flat by my own past. A miscellaneous Caucasian man sat down at the next table with his teenage son. His presence, his shape, the sound of his voice reminded me of a man I once knew, and brought an immediate and palpable reaction. It has been a long time since I have felt that panic rising in my throat, the crushing, heart-racing suffocation as my body remembers before my mind does.

Then come unbidden images flashing through the corridors of my mind like a Technicolor slide show. The little red tennis shoes half hidden by matching crumpled overalls on the floor…the slow-motion spin of ceiling fan overhead, the cigarette dangling from unshaven lips.

In a moment, I am transported from a little Thai restaurant with my husband to a cabin by the lake with a man I never should have known, half-a-world and a lifetime away. He owned a bait shop that stank of wriggling worms, decomposing earth and stale tobacco.

Although I would like to find some flowery description for him there is really no other way to describe 'the bait shop guy' as anything other than icky. My open resistance and rejection of him did not result in a reprieve in that little lakeside cabin. Instead, my rebellion earned a harsh punishment that was laid upon an innocent party, a beloved pet. The animal lay gutted and gasping, eyes bulging with terrified pain as the bait shop guy savagely claimed what he had paid for.

Even still, my defiance of the exploitation I was enduring lived on and sometimes manifested itself in outrageous ways. One subsequent occasion, I could not resist the urge to clamp my jaws down on the man paying for my attention. I did not want what he offered and so I bit what was put in my mouth with a fearsome tenacity. It was quite unfortunate for him that my two front teeth, missing for most of 1st grade had come back in beaver-like, sharp and too big for my mouth. I still remember with some measure of satisfaction the metallic taste of blood and him squealing like a stuck pig until a blow to my right temple caused me to see stars and loosen my bite.

The consequences for my actions that time were even more costly than a sacrificed pet and nothing would be gained by detailing the brutality of that punishment here. Suffice it to say that Ralph was a cruel schoolmaster, and the education I received from him was unforgettable. I learned through a series of brutal lessons not to fight and not to cry. Resistance was completely unacceptable and it alone was the only unforgivable sin. These were hard lessons, not only because of their cruelty but because I was and I am unwaveringly stubborn. Perhaps that wildly, defiant spirit that refused to yield in the face of fear is a gift from God. It most certainly is a gift that allowed me to survive years of the unthinkable, but also a gift that on more than one occasion nearly cost me my life. The double-edged sword of a courageous, rebel soul is a dangerous gift indeed.

Over the years of my trauma and abuse Ralph invested much time and energy in training me to submit on cue and attempting to subdue my rebellion. So when he took me from my antique brass bed in the middle of a summer night in 1981, he expected nothing but the obedient prized-possession that he had worked so hard to create. It might be said however, that on that particular night, I woke up on the wrong side of the bed.

He carried me into my grandmother's beautiful rose-colored bathroom where a warm bath was waiting. The walls were plastered with floral wallpaper in the latest fashion and a rainbow of ornate crystal perfume bottles glistened on the counter while she slept soundly just down the hall.

I allowed Ralph to undress me and put me into the pink enamel bathtub, moving robotically, as if still dreaming. But when he began to wash me, I woke from peaceful sleep to the nightmare unfolding. Initially, I just used my small hands to push away his invading roughness. He laughed as he easily thwarted my attempts at self-protection and my anger rose. I wanted to be asleep in my bed. I did not want his attention and despite all previous lessons learned, I threw caution to the wind and fought back. Someone from the outside looking in might observe that I was, by my actions, asking him to kill me; that I was in fact, trying to die instead of live. Maybe they would be right.

Try to give a feral cat a bubble bath, and you might have some small illustration of what ensued. I was a skinny, nine-year-old child but in that moment, remarkably untamed. I was clawing and thrashing wildly to escape the clutches of my captor. I kicked and I spit and I hit. I cussed like a sailor using combinations of foul language that most certainly would make your ears burn. I spewed my vehement and dangerous words at him like a machine gun assault. His laughter suddenly froze cold when my fingernails made contact and slashed the left side of his stubble-whiskered jaw, leaving two jagged lines of blood in his sagging flesh. It was then that the game turned deadly.

With his left hand closing around my throat he pushed me under the water, quickly silencing my rebellion. Still, I fought valiantly. As I tried to scream under the splashing water, my mouth, my throat, and my lungs filled. I clawed at his arm fighting for survival...or fighting to be killed. With wide eyes, I could see the hazy image of his dangerous smile through the moving window of water. He pulled me upright. Whether he did so in a moment of mercy or only to protect his investment, I will never know. With his iron grip remaining on my slender neck, I choked and vomited water. While gasping for air, my defiance grew and I uttered another long string of expletives. And back under the water I went. The back of my head slammed forcefully on the bottom of the bathtub as my grandfather struggled for control. My lungs burned aching for air and my soul ached longing for freedom as the edges of reality started growing dark. The image of his face distorted and faded into a gray blur as my flailing arms grew still. I don't know how long he held me under the water.

I do not know how long it takes to drown a child. I do know that I faded into a deep and peaceful warmth as the world went black. When I woke up sometime later I was dressed in my white lacy nightgown, hair still wet. Somewhere in the unconscious in-between, Ralph had dressed me and delivered me to a den of lions. Not one predator was waiting for me that night but several. Fully awake, with a belly still sloshing with water, I had no more fight. I had no more tears. It would be more than 10 years before I ever dared to fight again.

It is in these moments of climbing towards freedom in my daily life with bruised heart and bloody fingertips, I am often trying gallantly to find where the next finger hold is. In the here and now, I can sometimes feel the flood coming on, tears to cleanse, tears to release, tears to open, tears to break down strongholds, tears that have most often been imprisoned.

God has accomplished many things in my life. His mercies continue to be made new every morning. I have been a witness to many beautiful victories. But in the stillness of morning quiet; I am made deeply aware of a significant failure on my part. I have not often allowed myself the luxury of crying.

Courage is an important gift, but crying is another. The ability to weep for what was lost does not lessen the beauty of redemption. Crying for the pain experienced in a fallen world does not weaken the Savior who entered into this world wrapped in flesh. We so easily put on plastic smiles like pre-formed Halloween masks.

Do you remember those masks that you would put on as a child to disguise your own face and in return would be rewarded with treats from friendly neighbors? Maybe yours had the face of a princess with sun-yellow, molded hair and pink stamped lips or maybe a superhero square chin and black slick hair. Unfortunately, many of us started pretending at a young age and we have never stopped. We try to speak happy words through the little plastic slit all the while hiding the reality of sweaty brokenness underneath. These masks do not bring us freedom and healing nor do they glorify God.

The Bible says that the Truth will set us free. Sometimes the truth is that we need to weep. And by weep I mean letting loose the tear-your-clothes-sit-in-dust-and-ashes, wild cleansing tears. Tears like those shed in a garden called Gethsemane on a dark night 2,000 years ago. Gethsemane literally translates to a "place of crushing," and all who walk the face of this spinning sphere will experience it in one way or another.

The crushing comes in a variety of ways, but it always comes. We are crushed by loss, by betrayal, by disease, by bitterness. We are sometimes crushed by our own choices and the consequences of our sin. We must cry for all that has been lost, cry out for all the times that the dark won the day. We need to take off the plastic smiles and be real with ourselves and with one another.

A close friend once told me, "Jenni, girls fight with their tears." She was right. Crying can break chains that have long since held us captive. Sometimes crying is the most courageous act. The Truth that sets us free may very well come when the dam gives way to a torrential flood of a thousand unshed tears.

If I could give you a gift right now, I would hand you a sledgehammer and a box of Kleenex. Let us break down our walls. Can we be authentic? Can you and I be all we were created to be? We are made in the image of a wild, passionate, creator God. He is a Lion, He is a warrior. You and I, dear One, we are chips off of the old block. Even in the snot-dripping, puffy-faced broken, I invite you to take off your mask and I will take off mine. Let us be dangerous, be passionate, be courageous, be like Him, and be His.

CHAPTER 7

Questions from 3ʳᵈ Grade

Hiding under a bed or in the cool shadows of a small closet is where I felt the most at home. My favorite place to hide was an old wooden trunk that stored antique quilts in cedar-scented silence. Like a rabbit running from the fox, I was always scrambling and scurrying to burrow into shadowy escape. I sought refuge by trying to become invisible in small spaces and silent corners of darkness. I desperately hoped to remain unseen by the predators prowling, feeding on terror. Tragically, my reprieve would only last as long as the sun remained high. With the approach of darkness, so came the demand. I sometimes wonder how much the men were persuaded to spend to have a knobby-kneed child fulfill their sinister sexual fantasies. Could the price they paid, ever in any small measure, reflect what their lust cost me? I think not.

At 9 years old, I should have been exploring the farm and laughing with friends over silly things boys do. I should have been trying to outrun playground kisses. Instead, I learned exactly how to submit to a grown man with as little pain as possible. Who has the right to school a child in this fashion? I should have been innocent and naïve to the horrors that one person can inflict on another. Instead, I was destined to question every outstretched hand through the lens of torturous abuse. Who has the right to steal a child's innocence with violence? In third grade, I should have been wrestling with memorizing my times tables, instead of wrestling to keep my screams silent. Who has the right to imprison another's voice? I should have dreamed of a future but instead I dwelt day and night in a living nightmare. Who has the right to trample the dream of a child?

Perhaps I should pray for those men's repentance, their forgiveness, but in third grade I found a different prayer to pray. Mrs. Revoir made sure that every student in her class at St. Paul Lutheran School memorized the Apostles' Creed. For many kids, the words may have seemed obsolete and been no more significant than reciting the mandated lists of U.S. states and capitals. For me, the Apostles' Creed became a fragile lifeline.

The words themselves held no magic power that could hold back the crashing tides of lust and greed, but in the midst of a tsunami of violence, that prayer anchored my heart to something, to Someone greater. A rote prayer could not hold the power of life and death, but I believe it did hold the power to keep me sane. In the dark quiet I repeated it over and over each night until sleep ultimately overcame my resistance.

I believe in God, the Father almighty,
Creator of heaven and earth,
and in Jesus Christ, his only Son, our Lord,
who was conceived by the Holy Spirit,

born of the Virgin Mary, suffered under Pontius Pilate,
was crucified, died and was buried; he descended into hell;
on the third day he rose again from the dead;
he ascended into heaven,
and is seated at the right hand of God the Father almighty;
from there he will come to judge the quick and the dead.
I believe in the Holy Spirit, the holy catholic church,
the communion of saints, the forgiveness of sins,
the resurrection of the body, and life everlasting.

Time after time, I prayed the Apostles' Creed in defiance of my reality. It became a mantra, a child's battle cry written in ancient liturgy. Despite all of the evidence in my life that pointed to the contrary, I steadfastly believed there was a God, a Creator and an Almighty Father. I believed that Jesus came. I believed He suffered. I believed He knew the depths of hell. I believed He would come back for me and that He would judge the quick and the dead. I believed there would be life everlasting. I believed it because I was already personally acquainted with Him. Again and again He had come for me in the black oblivion of my own personal hell.

Can two truths that appear diametrically opposed exist in one space? I believe the life that God has permitted me to survive bears witness that they do. Standing on one side, I could use my own blood poured out and finger paint for you a picture of rape and torture that spanned 13 years. At the same time, I bear unwavering testimony of my allegiance to the One who never left me. That these two truths exist in one space, in one body and one mind is a paradox. But the fact that our minds cannot grasp the two sides at once does not change their veracity.

Perhaps in your life thus far, you have not yet experienced a significant trauma or loss. Oh, how I praise God for those of you whom that is true. I wish I could pledge to you a safe future as well. But we live in a fallen world and the Bible assures us and life affirms that we will all face suffering. There are a growing number of teachers and pastors with a skewed theology that promises you will be comfortable, wealthy and healthy, that those are your rights as a Christian. "Children of God are meant to live in victory," they will tell you from a pulpit built on a glittering catafalque.

It is not that I disagree with a life of victory. It is undeniably your destiny to overcome whatever you have faced and whatever the future holds. What I vehemently disagree with, is the context. The health and wealth preachers suggest that if you are struggling it is because of lack of faith. They bandage broken hearts with dirty Band-Aids, telling you that you are meant to be happy. The message that you should not be sick or struggling financially, or in the depths of depression as a Christian is not only blatantly false, but it offers no comfort at all to those who find themselves there.

While there is immeasurable and ultimate joy in victory, there is rarely happiness on a battlefield. The truth is that war is the context of the victory promised to the children of God. Men pinned down by the enemy in a firefight are not daydreaming about the future. If they are going to live through the battle, their focus must be singular. They and their comrades are under attack and there is an enemy that must be defeated at all cost. With hearts pounding in their ears and sweat pouring down their necks, warriors must remain hypervigilant. There will be a time for celebration later. For now, they are fighting and some of them are dying and some of them are surviving and that is victory.

Victory, by definition, is the act of defeating an enemy in battle or competition. Triumph and conquest do not come from a place of ease or luxury. My own struggle for victory inspired me to write this poem. It is my cringe-worthy alternate view of victory, true and battle worn. The scene is one in which a warrior has been severely wounded in battle and his only hope for survival is a battlefield amputation.

Leather strap between clenched teeth
Anguished cries are stifled
Anesthesia of ancient warrior

Tourniquet squeezes hard
A line drawn, living flesh
Excruciating wound seeping death

Suffering too great to bear
It must be torn away
Survival through a hideous cut

Battle weary, weakness comes
Bravery on display
Hot knife sears muscle, saw grating bone

Who would ever imagine
No end to agony?
For valiant battle to come to this

But screams of pain testify
Across the fields of death
That LIFE rages on
And faithful are the wounds of a Friend.

We all face suffering and trauma as an inevitable part of life. The question is what will we do when we are faced with unanswerable pain? Perhaps you did not see with your eyes Jesus come for you as your hurt unfolded. Maybe you did not feel His arms around you or His quivering strength restrained as He held His unfathomable wrath at bay. Maybe all you have seen is the blood and the very real losses of battle. That does not mean He was not there or that He is not just.

Whatever you have gone through, to whatever depths of the abyss your heart has plummeted, you are here now to read these words. You have survived thus far. Your survival and mine is not an accident, nor is it a tribute to the resiliency of the human spirit alone. Your survival and mine is a tribute to the One in whose image we were made. Trauma is nothing if not blinding. It blinds us to who we are and who we were made to be. Most often, trauma blinds us to who God is, and therein lies the greatest tragedy. Healing comes in remembering the ancient truth that is carved into our very DNA. The surgeon in my poem above is tasked with amputating a limb that is beyond saving. The warrior has nothing to dull the agonizing pain but a leather strap clinched between his teeth. The warrior could view the surgeon as his enemy but nothing is further from the truth. The surgeon is his friend, he has not only witnessed the battle but fought alongside in it. The only hope for healing comes in cutting away the wound. The surgeon is not the enemy, but rather the Healer. Sometimes it is shattering pain that testifies the loudest of final victory. A victory that will someday be complete and full of joy.

"I believe in God, the Father almighty, Creator of heaven and earth…" There is a Creator God, the Almighty. You and I, we together, are made in His image. Freedom comes in walking out this truth in a world that appears upside down and inside out. He who was and is and is to come has by His very nature and character never abandoned us. The truth of this paradox is not measured in the ability of our blind eyes to see it. The truth of it is measured in our ability to defiantly believe in the goodness and faithfulness of God despite any

and all physical evidence to the contrary. Some skeptics belittle this type of faith, calling it a crutch, a sign of mental or physical weakness. For those of you wounded warriors reading this book, I beg to differ. This type of faith is a sign of strength that is no less than supernatural. To believe the best anyway, to hope in love, to entrust ourselves fully to Someone unseen and for our souls to take flight and rejoice even in the midst of gut-wrenching trauma, these are not only evidences of divine strength but of the Divine, Himself at work in and through us.

Memorizing the Apostles' Creed in the third grade was the gift that anchored my soul to God. Even still, in the eight years that followed, the exploitation I continued to endure would repeatedly shipwreck and nearly obliterate that faith. There would come a time that the violence would cause me to walk away from Jesus and everything I believed about Him, but that is for another chapter. For this moment, let us focus instead on the strange gifts of grace that bind us to the Eternal.

There is only One anchor that holds fast in any storm. His name is Jesus. He alone is strong enough and brave enough to weather whatever you have faced or are now facing or will face in the future. Perhaps my saying that makes you feel angry or grieved. It is okay. Push back against that which provokes and challenges you. Your destiny is victory because you were made to fight.

We are in a war, dear one, so fight it out. Before you put this down and walk away I have one more question. I have been honest with you, now it is your turn. What has been your anchor? In what does your strength lie? Has it been sufficient and in the end, will it be enough?

CHAPTER 8

An End and a Beginning

In my ears I hear the frantic crying cease and the haunting melody of "Hush little baby, don't say a word…" begin. It is me singing, I am nine years old. I can smell the rich, dark, earthy smell of fresh blood. I can feel the weight of a cold dead baby cradled in the crook of my scrawny left arm. She is so very cold and so very little. I hold her tightly to my chest rocking, singing her a lullaby that she cannot hear. I cannot make her warm. We are both cold away from the fire. If I look I can see the huge wound in her chest, but if I hold her just right the edges come together and she looks almost whole. Her eyes are vacant, an empty reflection of the bonfire. I am not in use, in the midst of a drunken orgy. I am mercifully invisible just now…a naked little girl, rocking and singing to a lifeless baby in a world all our own.

I remained in that distant other world for several days after that event. After my worried mother picked me up from my grandparents' house, she took me straight to a trusted family friend. Grandpa

Dennis was a pediatrician that lived next door to our funeral home. Unlike the other men I knew, he was a good and a gentle man, one in whose lap I could sit without fear or hesitation. He examined me in his avocado-and-daisy colored kitchen.

"It looks like she is in a catatonic state. Do you know what happened?" He asked my mother quietly. She shook her head, "No, I have no idea," was her honest reply.

"Well, I suggest give it a week. If she doesn't come out of it on her own in seven days we will put her in the hospital."

Over the years of growing up in exploitation, my body was used repeatedly for sex, for the making of child pornography and even on occasion for ritual abuse. The single snapshot glimpse of horror above, glaringly captured with flash too bright, was in the context of the latter. The memories of that week remain for me surreal and fragmented. The customer is always right and my grandfather made sure the men always got what they paid for. In this instance, what was required was almost more than my fragile mind could endure. Almost.

In the days that followed, I remember being wrapped in a blanket sitting next to the window listening to what was going on, but somehow I remained locked within myself. Unable to respond with either words or tears, I sat and rocked myself steadily back and forth, back and forth. Unapproachable and untouchable, I hid deeply within myself. When weariness took over, I would drift off to sleep humming, "Hush little baby," only to wake up sometime later screaming.

My parents had several discussions about what might have happened while I was at my grandparents' house. When they tired of speculating and talking themselves in circles, my mom sat with me in the quiet with impotent tears dripping off of her chin. A few days into the bizarre wake, one of their discussions escalated into a heated argument that ended with my mom taking a vehement stand, "I don't know what happened but I know for sure that she won't ever go back there!" A door slammed, something shattered, and I broke free from the land of the shadows.

It had been three and a half days since my mother had come to pick me up from my grandparents and found me in a catatonic state. Whether my parents were afraid of knowing the truth themselves or afraid that it might cause a relapse for me to recount it, I do not know. I do know that after my soul rejoined my body, my parents did not ever ask what had happened. And in all fairness to them, I know beyond a shadow of a doubt, that if they had asked, there is no way in heaven or in hell I would have told them. Never. No not ever.

What I could not possibly know then and would not know for many years to come, was how God was working to affect my rescue during that bloody week in the summer of 1981. His sovereignty was revealed over a cup of spicy red rooibos tea.

When a new friend invited me over to get acquainted in the fall of 2006, neither she nor I had any idea that the meeting had been orchestrated by God nearly 25 years before. Picture it with me for a moment. Imagine God on His throne, leaning forward, lifting a hand and hushing the angels who worship ceaselessly before Him. Watch the Most Holy One calling attention to the dramatic scene unfolding below in a warm Colorado kitchen. See with me the witnesses of heaven watching breathlessly as these pieces finally fell into place.

At that point, Susan and I were only acquaintances who had come to work for the same organization. We had led vastly different lives, lived different stories, and spent the majority of our lives in different parts of the U.S. We each had our own personal triumphs and tragedies, yet by God's design, we had landed at a common table.

We began to break the ice that afternoon with the customary nice-ties. "How many kids do you have? How long have you lived here? How did you come to work for this organization?" As our conversation grew warm and our tea grew cold I felt the presence of the Holy Spirit pressing in on me. He was compelling me to share something from my past, a particular event that I had not ever spoken aloud. Internally a war began as I argued against His direction. But as you might have experienced, God has not ever lost a wrestling match. So with fear and trepidation, I treaded carefully into the dark caverns of memory. I told my new friend that I felt strongly I needed to share something with her, but I had not ever told it to anyone before. With an open heart and indulgent eyes, she welcomed my story. Her eyes were the color of a crisp Colorado sky and I found my wings and my voice. Freedom beckoned to me yawning and stretching.

I cracked open the door of vulnerability by telling Susan that I had been abused as a child. When she did not flinch, I proceeded a little more boldly into the deep.

"My grandfather sold me into prostitution when I was four years old," I said with trembling voice. She listened with rapt attention as I told her that I had experienced something so devastating when I was nine years old that it had left me in a clinical catatonic state for three days. As I started to unfold the details of that trauma, tears leapt to her eyes. She held up her hand and stopped me short.

"The summer of '81." She said quietly. "Did this happen to you in the summer of '81?"

Quickly I calculated, "Yes, I was nine years old in the summer of '81."

Her fugitive tears broke free from all constraint, and Susan explained.

"I know what happened to you that night, here's how... In the summer of '81 I was a young mother living in Texas. One night I had a terrible nightmare. When I woke up I was overwhelmed with fear, I couldn't stop crying and could not escape the images that had played out in my dream. What happened seemed more real to me awake than it had seemed while I was sleeping. After several minutes I was overwhelmed with the feeling that what I had seen was not just a dream but it was actually happening to a little girl somewhere in the world…at that very moment. I got down on my knees on the side of the bed and began crying out to God on behalf of that little girl. I was praying with all of my heart for protection, for healing, for deliverance, for justice for her wherever she was. For days afterward, she did not escape my thoughts and I prayed for her nearly continuously. In the first months following that night I prayed for her every single day. As time passed, my prayers grew less frequent, but I prayed whenever she came to mind…several times a week initially, a couple of times a month later. Just yesterday, I was compelled again to pray for that little girl, to pray for you."

And in those moments she gave voice to the trauma that I had not ever dared to speak aloud. She knew where I had been and what had happened. She had been devastated and compelled by the secrets of that night for 25 years.

Why a young mother over 600 miles away would be awakened in the middle of the night with the nightmare that was my life, I cannot begin to explain. That she would be compelled to her knees urgently pleading on behalf of a child whom she had never met is a testament to the power and grace of a Living God. When my tears were cruelly ensnared somewhere in the in-between, Susan set them free. Her tears flowed unrestrained in the dark. She cried for me when I could not. When my tongue became a prisoner of war, mute and powerless, Susan spoke. She prayed fervently for me, giving voice to the unthinkable. God heard both her prayers whispering and my silence shouting. He heard and He entered in. That week in the summer of '81 represented both an end and a beginning.

That particular event was an end to the extended stays with my grandparents. My grandfather would never again have lengthy periods of time in which to perpetrate his wickedness. Violence does not require much time, but obscuring the evidence does. A rape can be accomplished in the time it takes a second hand to travel, trip, skip, ticking around a clock face 4 or 5 times. But for the bleeding to stop, for the bruises to heal, for the happy child to return to the vacant and subdued flesh, these all require time.

After Susan's impassioned prayers and my mother's adamant declarations, my grandfather would never again be afforded the same luxury of time. That was a gift from God representing an unmistakable mercy. I wish that was the end of the story. How badly I wish I could pen the words, "they lived happily ever after," here and now. Unfortunately, that was not yet to be. While it is true that the bloody week in the summer of '81 brought an end to some of the exploitation, there was a new beginning as well.

In July of that year, a few short months after my tenuous deliverance, my father came to the end of himself. For most of his life, alcohol had been a selfish and capricious mistress. When my father found that she could never satisfy the brokenness within him, he walked away once and for all. There were 30 days of inpatient treatment, and then the 12 steps, meetings and sponsors. The triad of AA, Ala-non and Ala-teen (although I was only 9 years old) promised us each a new way of life. In recovery, he and my mother decided that they needed to move away and have a fresh start. It seemed best to them to begin again in a place where they would have the support of family. So that summer found us closing the 3-hour distance that had always separated my home from my grandparents. I walked away from the funeral home with great heaving sobs and into the catacombs.

We settled a few miles away from the farm, the slaughterhouse, and the many other crime scenes of my repeated assaults. What my grandfather then lacked in leisurely time was more than made up for by his near constant access.

His strategy was forced to change. I would need to become even more submissive. It was imperative that I be taught to resist less. The perpetrators would have to be held to a higher standard, accountable to leaving less damage in their lust-filled wake, another small gift of mercy. Physical force became less necessary as psychological control increased. And so I grew in wisdom and stature with lessons of submission carved into the sinews of my being. The violence became random, then sporadic. Exploitation at the whim of my grandfather became the exception rather than the rule. I never knew when I fell asleep if I would awaken in the presence of the enemy. And that, in and of itself, represents its own kind of horror.

Yet, God had, in fact, protected me. He had awoken Susan in the middle of the night many a time to intercede for my life and my sanity. He had answered, but the deliverance would not yet be complete. Even now, I am still found often longing for the promised happily ever after. And even now, I occasionally receive notes from Susan still whispering prayers for my continued healing. God intervened. He wound the thread of Susan's life around the thread of mine and into the great tapestry of His story.

Often, it appears that our prayers go unheard. Like caged birds, they flutter on crippled wings from our mouths only to batter hopelessly against the invisible bars of our captivity. It sometimes feels as if our prayers travel no further than the ceiling above us having imparted no significant impact on either the physical or the spiritual realm. '*It appears...it feels*' are the operational words here. This is a mystery, one I cannot possibly explain but Paul gives us a clue in his second letter to the Corinthians. He explains in 2 Corinthians 5:7, "We walk by faith, not by sight." This is not a mindless faith of a hapless sheep. It is anything but naïve. It is rather that here in the shadowlands, our eyes become irrelevant to the seeing.

I could not see God acting on my behalf when I was 9 years old, and Susan had no way to measure if or how her prayers were being answered. Neither of us would have any evidence at all of the outcome of those prayers for more than two decades. But by the will of God, through the sacrificial death of Jesus and in the power of the Holy Spirit, Susan and I were brought together over a cup of tea. Now I have this assurance, this hope that is not based on what I feel and never on how things appear, but rather a hope that is fixed on Him who is called Faithful.

Make no mistake, dear one, prayer was never meant to be a cosmic vending machine in which I deposit my two cents worth and life change is magically dispensed. Prayer matters, but not because of how or when the answers manifest in our physical realm. Prayer may or may not change our circumstances but it always serves to change us. The primary purpose of prayer is accomplished only as much as it draws us ever deeper into intimate relationship with Jesus. It is this intimate conversation that permits us bold entry into the most holy throne room, and this intimacy allows us to fearlessly approach the throne of grace. In coming close we begin to see with eyes of faith. And it is with this faith that I can conclude, on a preponderance of unseen evidence, that prayer matters. It matters to us and it matters to God.

"Of course," you might say. We can all nod our assent to the fact that prayer matters in the general sense. But, dear one, does it matter to you personally? Do you believe that you are loved at the very core of your being? Do you pray as if you are valued and heard? Do you pray as if someone's life, their very destiny, hangs in the balance? When you pray, do you expect answers or do you expect a deeper relationship and greater understanding of Him?

Spend a few minutes here, ask yourself these questions. Listen quietly for the answers. Draw near to Jesus, lay bare the deep dark of your heart, talk, weep, shout, wrestle if you must. But whatever you do, please do not leave this space until you have begun a new conversation with the One who died so you could be heard. I double dog dare you.

CHAPTER 9

Ultimate Betrayal

I met Jesus in the strangest places while I was growing up, and it was rarely where one would expect. He was inexplicably distant from me when I occasionally sat in a Catholic Mass with my nanny. I came away from those ornate services feeling in awe of the holiness of God, but that impression did nothing to draw me near to Him. His gilded body nailed eternally to a cross hanging over the altar seemed nothing like the Living Jesus, Strong and Gentle, who had come for me in the backseat of my grandfather's car when I was four years old.

Don't get me wrong, my experiences in the Catholic Church were not negative ones. In fact, I remember those times with a great deal of tenderness and nostalgia. Unlike some other people, my experiences there were not damaging or abusive, they were just wholly inadequate. During my elementary years, I also regularly heard stories about Jesus as I sat dutifully between Ralph and my bejeweled grandmother in their small town Christian church. Those stories, however, were so distant from the reality of my life that they fell on my ears distorted and rambling, as if spoken in some foreign tongue. I did not encounter Jesus in their church either.

When I was fourteen, a friend of my parents invited our family to visit her church. Kaye had known my mother since their teenage years and their long history lent credibility to the invitation. My dad had been sober for five years by then, but had not yet nailed down who he believed his "higher power" to be. So the next Sunday, we dressed up and walked into a tiny rural church in nowhere, Missouri. It was there, that I heard the gospel preached in its beautiful entirety for the very first time.

Brother Wayne preached from his heart, and the words bypassed my ears and fell directly onto my soul. He explained with an unfamiliar mix of sensitivity and passion that we have all sinned and that we were all in need of a Savior. On this point, he and I were in total agreement. Sin and I were intimately acquainted. I had plumbed the depths of sin at its ugliest. Everything within me vibrated with the dark sting of it. His words exposed my wounds to the light and at the same time promised me a hope of rescue. When Brother Wayne introduced Jesus, a suffering Servant, the Lamb who was slain, I was finally given a formal introduction to the One who had been wooing me for years.

As was traditional in the buckle of the Midwestern Bible belt, at the close of the church service an invitation to respond was given. That means that those in the congregation who were so moved, actually got up out of their seats and, in front of God and everybody, went down to the altar to pray and publicly invite Jesus to be their Lord and Savior. As humiliating and offensive as this might seem in our current cultural context, believe me when I tell you that shackles and chains could not have held me in that lumpy rust-colored pew.

My heart flew in pursuit of freedom and I am fairly sure that it landed in throbbing surrender at the altar before my feet had the chance to catch up. There was a spiritual transaction that day, one of eternal significance. I knew that I desperately needed a Savior and I believed beyond a shadow of doubt that Jesus was that One, the One and Only. In that moment, I surrendered myself to Jesus, the One who had died not only to take away the guilt of every sin that I had ever committed but also to take away the shame and pain of every brutal crime that had been committed against me.

Not long after, I followed through on that decision and was baptized in a nearby river. It was July 14, 1986, and I was 14 years old. Trusting myself to be plunged underwater by Brother Wayne's hands was a monumental task but I desperately ached to be made clean. In this case, my desire outweighed my fear. With a deep breath I went under the cool water, willingly burying my past, my sin and my blood-stained shame. I can still remember the late afternoon sunlight dancing on the rippling waters as I rose spotless to a new life with a virgin hope. I was once more made innocent and my tender faith was untried. Warm, dripping wet and alive we carpooled to the church for a potluck dinner. When Kaye and Brother Wayne and others who had gathered in celebration, promised that the old had passed away and the new had come I believed them.

I believed them all the way up until the moment that my grandfather came for me again. I learned quickly that the saving grace of Jesus did not guard me from the lust and profit of my grandfather's trade.

The worst violation happened the following summer when I was 15. I will be as gentle with the details here as possible but perhaps you should prepare yourself. Please take a moment and invite Jesus to give you spiritual eyes to see and to guard your heart so that you can bear my story with the tenderness it deserves. Either that, or perhaps you might just skip ahead to the next chapter. You have permission. You can stay with me here or you can go.

When you are ready, and not a moment before, you can move with me into the past.

Please forgive my improper use of grammatical tense in the following; it seems that I can only tell this part of the story in present tense. No matter how many years it has been and how much healing has transpired, a part of me crystallized and is still on some level held captive in the following few hours of time.

There is a hanging light with a big metal cone shade, it glares in the darkness. I am 15 years old and in the slaughterhouse. I am lying, flat on my back, on a rough, blood-stained, wooden table. There are black leather belts that are around my wrists and around my neck, restraining me and restricting my breath. My legs are propped up against some sort of makeshift stirrups, they are pinned to wooden boards with 2 black belts cinched down tightly on each leg. I am screaming. I am literally screaming bloody murder.

I was young and I was ignorant. Before I had known or understood, my grandfather had figured out that I was pregnant. This presented an enormous problem for him, as at 15 years old, my parents had not yet permitted me to date. Only rape or immaculate conception could explain my condition. The first being entirely unpalatable and the second impossible, he knew he was at risk of being found out.

"How Great Thou Art" is playing loudly and repeatedly. Ralph is singing along. There is another man standing between my legs. He is providing a gruesome solution to my grandfather's problem and removing the evidence of my exploitation one piece at a time. Together, they are aborting my child.

There are times and places that trauma is so severe that, for a time, it tears through the veil. In that space, the spiritual realm becomes as clear and as real as the physical realm. So I am neither being imaginative nor allegorical when I tell you that Jesus, in the resurrected flesh, is a primary's player in this scene. In fact, he is my midwife. He stands at my head, shushing me. A strong scarred hand holds firmly on either side of my tear streaked face. I do not shush, but keep screaming at the pain, wild and uninhabitable.

"Look at me," Jesus whispers. "Look at me!" He demands. "Stay right here with me. I AM here, I've got you, baby. I am here....I've got you."

Jesus is wearing blue jeans and a casual white button down shirt, wrinkled and untucked with sleeves rolled up haphazardly once at the cuffs. He wipes my sweat-soaked brow and my tears with the hem of his shirt. The Jesus I know is like that, authentic and unadorned. I felt his touch as surely as I felt the invasion of the butcher.

In the shadowy corner on my right, I can see three men towering. No, but they are not men, they are more than men. They are angels, gladiator-strong and battle-scarred. Although perhaps some do, these three angels do not appear to have wings. They must be nearly nine feet tall and are standing at attention. Their hands are on their swords at the ready. The three stand waiting for the command to act with a righteous and fiery wrath barely restrained. I am still screaming and though I cannot see their faces I sense that they are crying. Jesus, throws his head back and lets out the savage roar of a Lion. The terrifying sound of his grief and pain shatters the darkness. His voice thunders, "Father God! How will she ever understand? How can she ever understand this?"

My soul shakes with His passion and His prayer. Time skips and jumps. The violence against me shutter steps to a halt for the briefest second. Jesus bows His head over me again. He smells like sunshine on the sea. His face is close to mine. His ragged breath is on my ear. He whispers impossible comfort as His own tears drip, drip, splash down onto my face intermingling with my own.

One of the warrior angels steps up beside me, and in his hands he is holding the tiniest baby against a bare, battle-scarred chest. His arms are muscled; his skin is a beautiful burnished bronze. He has leather and metal gauntlets on his wrists that go halfway up his massive forearms.

Jesus tells me to open my eyes and to look. "Shhhh, shhhhh, look. Look at your baby. She is safe. She is beautiful. Look, her name is Zayda, the lucky one."

The angel loosens the grip of his massive hands, just enough for me to catch a glimpse of her, the tiny, tiny baby. She is flesh of my flesh and blood of my blood. In his hands, she is pink and whole and alive. She is 15 weeks old. Suddenly, in a rush of wind the angel shoots up through the roof. He and the baby, and the very last shred of evidence of anything holy or innocent in me, are all gone. The desolation is profound.

Zayda truly is the "lucky one" and I am not. I am left strapped to the table. The procedure is done but the torture is not. I do not know what they are saying but Ralph is laughing. He steps up to the table and forces himself into my emptiness. When he is satisfied, the other man, the one who murdered my child and part of my soul, follows Ralph's lead. In the span of an hour, I lose my first conceived child and survive being raped by two men. When they finally step away from the scene and into the darkness they are both sticky with my blood from the waist down. Somewhere in the night I stopped screaming. Although "How Great Thou Art," has long since stopped playing, Ralph still whistles the haunting refrain. The cassette player clicks loudly its frustration when the tape reaches the end of itself.

Sometime later, I climb the stairs to my room slowly, a pink floral bath towel wadded up between my legs. Unexpectedly, I am ancient, hunched like an old woman over the immeasurable pain. That night I slept long but fitfully, feverish from shock and blood loss. I dreamed of fighting off the men. I dreamed of defending someone small and weak. In my dreams, I am always running...running far and fast. But in my dreams and in real life I was never fast enough; they always won.

When I woke up, I was faced with a paradox, unknowable and unsolvable. Is God all good or is God all powerful? In my mind and my experience I could not grasp the possibility that He could be both. I could not reconcile the two ideas. My circumstances seemed to prove that either God is all good but He is weak or that He is all powerful but He not good. Either there is a good God who saw my hurt and my pain and wanted to protect me but was too weak to do so, or there is an all-powerful God that had within Him the strength to defend me but did not care to do so. This profound contradiction would drive me away from God for years to come. I could neither bring myself to trust God's goodness nor His power.

Jesus was right when He prayed for me on that dark night. I did not understand. I could not possibly understand this. I had known treachery at the hands of men my entire life, but this was the first time I had felt betrayed by God. I had been in church for more than a year already. I had gone to Sunday school every week and was there every time the doors were opened. I had earned gold stars for having memorized Bible verses. I read my Bible. I had learned to fast and to pray and to give. I had given my life to Him in childlike faith and naïve trust. I had done my part. But in spite of all of my striving and my genuine surrender, I still was not safe. For the first time in my life, Jesus' presence in the midst of my trauma was not sufficient. That He was there but did not intervene became for me the ultimate betrayal. I was 15 years old and had already survived 11 years of captivity. In my fragility and brokenness, I became convinced that rescue was not ever coming. This changed everything for me. I could not, no, I would not any longer trust God's goodness and nor would I trust His power.

And you, dear one, are you still here? If you have made it this far, you are mighty indeed. I am not referring to making it this far into my story, but making it this far in your own. What have your betrayals been? Can you itemize them? Who hurt you? Who left you? Where were you when you first believed in the possibility of God? What were the circumstances that conspired to steal your hope and your future? Have you found God to be sufficient to answer your suffering? Do you believe that God is all powerful and all good?

In old Western movies there is often an iconic scene, one in which the heroine has encountered some great trauma or loss. The cattle have been stolen or the outlaws have raided. You know the script. The cowboy hero is going to go after the villain, the white hat to conquer the black. But she is furious and she is afraid and in her despair she slaps the cowboy in the face. She pounds her fists on his chest. And the hero, he lets her. The sting of her strike does not cause him to pull away. He does not reject her or return the blows. The fact that he does not strike back does not compromise his strength. He stands immovable, holding her tightly until her pain is exhausted and she wilts into his arms.

Forgive me, it is a shallow allegory at best, grainy, black and white. The hero of our stories is a carpenter not a cowboy, but Jesus is the truest Hero nonetheless. He is immovable in the face of your struggle and your grief. He can take it. Not only will He not turn away but He will hold you with the fiercest love until you have spent every last ounce of your grief.

I was too blind to see this truth at 15 years old. It would take me years of rebellion and desert wandering to discover the only place my healing could ever be found. But if you would let me, I can save you the trip through the badlands. You do not have to run like I did. You have a choice. Here is the deal: No matter which road we take, the destination we are all secretly longing for is only ever found in Jesus. You can turn to Him. You can pound on his chest, you can pour out your grief, and His shoulders are strong enough to bear the weight of your rage and your bewilderment. Then when all of your emotion is finally spent you can crumple into the muscled arms of a Jewish carpenter. His arms have been outstretched and waiting for you for more than 2,000 years. Please, dear one, do not waste another minute.

CHAPTER 10

The Dark Years

It was with great reluctance that I turned from my faith. It did not happen all at once but instead my faith slowly grew cold in the face of an arctic wasteland of betrayals and disappointments. I waited for God to act. I believed that if God was, in fact, all good and all powerful, then the very least He could do was to let me die. But He failed me again and yet again. It was my grandfather who showed up instead. I pled with God to permit me to die, when He refused I grew angry. It was a final proof in a mounting pool of evidence I thought, of His profound carelessness.

From the outside looking in, no one would have known that I lived in two separate worlds. By day, I was a cheerleader and pushed myself to perfection, a straight A student in AP classes. I was popular and one of the "good girls." I had continued to go to church, became a leader in the youth group and even began teaching a Sunday school class of 1st graders. Like spreading a handmade wedding quilt on top of a bed of maggots, my high school years looked perfect but covered the stench of death. The outside was a picturesque façade of quaint beauty and it was only I, who knew the grotesque malevolence underneath.

I continued to read my Bible looking for whatever key I had missed. But something was very, very wrong, what I thought was promised was not at all what was delivered. Like the horse chasing the proverbial carrot on a stick I endlessly sought freedom but remained in captivity. I had been betrayed by men, betrayed by God and ultimately I found myself betrayed by a story that I found in the Bible.

In the book of Judges, chapter 19 there is a story that further drove in the nails crucifying my fragile faith. The story is about a re-spected religious leader in ancient Israel. He was a Levite by trade who owned a concubine. A concubine in this context was a female slave who functioned as a secondary wife or surrogate mother. Her owner would be called husband and he would enter into a contrac-tual son-in-law/father-in-law relationship with her father but she, as a slave, would not be afforded the status or legal rights and protec-tions of a wife. I will let you read the story for yourself. The Message version reads this way.

> **_Judges 19_** _It was an era when there was no king in Israel. A Levite, living as a stranger in the backwoods hill country of Ephraim, got himself a concubine, a woman from Bethlehem in Judah. But she quarreled with him and left, returning to her father's house in Bethlehem in Judah. She was there four months. Then her husband decided to go after her and try to win her back. He had a servant and a pair of donkeys with him. When he arrived at her father's house, the girl's father saw him, welcomed him, and made him feel at home. His father-in-law, the girl's father,_

*pressed him to stay. He stayed with him three days;
they feasted and drank and slept.*

*On the fourth day, they got up at the crack of dawn
and got ready to go. But the girl's father said to his
son-in-law, "Strengthen yourself with a hearty
breakfast and then you can go." So they sat down
and ate breakfast together.*

*The girl's father said to the man, "Come now, be my
guest. Stay the night—make it a holiday." The man
got up to go, but his father-in-law kept after him, so
he ended up spending another night.*

*On the fifth day, he was again up early, ready to go.
The girl's father said, "You need some breakfast."
They went back and forth, and the day slipped on as
they ate and drank together. But the man and his
concubine were finally ready to go. Then his father-
in-law, the girl's father, said, "Look, the day's almost
gone—why not stay the night? There's very little
daylight left; stay another night and enjoy yourself.
Tomorrow you can get an early start and set off
for your own place."*

*But this time the man wasn't willing to spend another
night. He got things ready, left, and went as far as
Jebus (Jerusalem) with his pair of saddled donkeys,
his concubine, and his servant. At Jebus, though, the
day was nearly gone. The servant said to his master,*

"It's late; let's go into this Jebusite city and
spend the night."

But his master said, "We're not going into any city of
foreigners. We'll go on to Gibeah." He directed his
servant, "Keep going. Let's go on ahead. We'll spend
the night either at Gibeah or Ramah."

So they kept going. As they pressed on, the sun finally
left them in the vicinity of Gibeah, which belongs to
Benjamin. They left the road there to spend the
night at Gibeah.

The Levite went and sat down in the town square, but
no one invited them in to spend the night. Then, late
in the evening, an old man came in from his day's
work in the fields. He was from the hill country of
Ephraim and lived temporarily in Gibeah where all
the local citizens were Benjaminites.

When the old man looked up and saw the traveler in
the town square, he said, "Where are you going?
And where are you from?"

The Levite said, "We're just passing through. We're
coming from Bethlehem on our way to a remote spot
in the hills of Ephraim. I come from there. I've just
made a trip to Bethlehem in Judah and I'm on my
way back home, but no one has invited us in for the
night. We wouldn't be any trouble: We have food and

straw for the donkeys, and bread and wine for the woman, the young man, and me—we don't need anything."

The old man said, "It's going to be all right; I'll take care of you. You aren't going to spend the night in the town square." He took them home and fed the donkeys. They washed up and sat down to a good meal.

They were relaxed and enjoying themselves when the men of the city, a gang of local hell-raisers all, surrounded the house and started pounding on the door. They yelled for the owner of the house, the old man, "Bring out the man who came to your house. We want to have sex with him."

He went out and told them, "No, brothers! Don't be obscene—this man is my guest. Don't commit this outrage. Look, my virgin daughter and his concubine are here. I'll bring them out for you. Abuse them if you must, but don't do anything so senselessly vile to this man."

But the men wouldn't listen to him. Finally, the Levite pushed his concubine out the door to them. They raped her repeatedly all night long. Just before dawn they let her go. The woman came back and fell at the door of the house where her master was sleeping. When the sun rose, there she was.

It was morning. Her master got up and opened the
door to continue his journey. There she was, his
concubine, crumpled in a heap at the door, her hands
on the threshold.

"Get up," he said. "Let's get going."
There was no answer. He lifted her onto his donkey
and set out for home. When he got home he took a
knife and dismembered his concubine—cut her into
twelve pieces. He sent her, piece by piece, throughout
the country of Israel.

It is not a story for Sunday school, is it? You are not going to see that one depicted on a flannel graph or painted in the church nursery. This story of brutality sucker punched me and left me gasping for breath. As a teenager still surviving in captivity, I could not wrap my mind around it.

Can you see the homeowner trying to reason with the gang? In essence he is saying, "Here, I will give you two for the price of one." Hear his words again, "No, brothers! Don't be obscene—this man is my guest. Don't commit this outrage. Look, my virgin daughter and his concubine are here. I'll bring them out for you. Abuse them if you must, but don't do anything so senselessly vile to this man."

"What?!?" my heart shouted at the injustice. "Take the girls and do what you want, but don't do anything so vile to this man." How dare he? What kind of father makes such a bargain?

Look over in the corner of the ancient home. See the concubine cowering there in the candlelit shadows, her eyes wild with fear. She has been a slave to one man's lust already, and she had run away from him one time that we know about. She knows full well the deal on the table and what is at stake. Can you see the Levite dragging her by her hair, and without compassion or mercy shoving her out the door? Hear the slamming door that seals her fate. It must have taken a lot of effort for a spineless man to push her out and barricade himself inside, but he managed. The girl was sacrificed and he was safe.

If you can bear it, enter into the story with me for just a moment more. Does our little concubine sister turn and claw at the locked door begging to be let back inside or does she turn and face the men? Does she fall to her knees weeping or does she take a deep breath and square her shoulders bracing herself? In different times and places, I have done of all of the above. I have fought. I have surrendered. I have wept and I have squared my shoulders. As I look at her I wonder, 'Which is nobler? Which is braver?' I wonder, 'Did she die well? What does it even mean to die well?'

As the unimaginable unfolds outside the house can you hear the taunting and jeers of the gang? Their savage laughter echoing in the darkness; human jackals devouring their prey. Can you hear her screaming, her pleading? Can you catch the moment that her screams grow silent and her soul flees into the night? I can and I do not exaggerate when I say that it both breaks my heart and it infuriates me.

How could God let this happen? And why did He see fit to put it in the Bible? This story rarely gets much attention. You may have been a Christian for many years and never have heard it. I, to this day, have never heard it preached from a pulpit, but it has been immortalized in Scripture nonetheless.

As a teenage survivor, what I came away with after having read this story, was that girls are expendable and that men must be satisfied and protected at all cost. The ruthless lust of the gang was satisfied. The homeowner was safe. The preacher was protected. The power paradigm did not shift, so all was well.

"All was well?! Really?!" I cannot string letters together fast enough to convey how profoundly betrayed I felt by this story. Even now, as I sit here writing to you, I am moved. I can feel my heart raging against the confines of my chest. We do not even know her name. I want to know her name!

If someone were to read only these few pages of this book they could easily conclude that I rejected God and may even be tempted to justify me in doing so. They would be correct but only in part. The lens in which I viewed this story was deeply distorted and I did reject God for a time. But keep reading, dear one. There is more to this story even though I would not come to understand it until I came to live in Peru more than 20 years later.

The healing balm of truth settled into my soul in a slum outside of Lima, Peru. The area is known as Jose Galvez. The 8' x 8' squatters homes that spread over the desert region are constructed of cardboard and scraps from the dump. It is a place of abject poverty and unrestrained crime. The streets are dangerous and theft is the norm. A woman cannot safely walk to the corner bakery unescorted by a man because violence is prevalent.

Yet Jose Galvez is where my husband, our 3 kids and I settled for a short season in early 2006. We had come as missionaries to support a local church in reaching and transforming their community with the gospel of Jesus.

It was my first experience living in another culture, and I was way out of my league in every respect. I could not shop for groceries alone and even if I could, I had no idea where to go. My Martha Stewart home-making skills left me ill prepared for how my neighbors fed their families. Sometimes buying live chickens in the local markets or on more dire days they chased down stray animals in the streets for dinner. Perhaps you are a bit more experienced than I, but I honestly did not have a clue how to turn a live chicken into something my family would eat nor was I anxious to serve cat for dinner. Additionally, I was pretty sure that if I went through the process of learning either of those culinary techniques, I would become a dedicated vegetarian for life. I prefer my meat shrink wrapped and resembling nothing of its former self. Needless to say, I avoided the live markets and the first few weeks we survived on peanut butter and jelly that we had brought from the States. Ultimately, I did learn how and where to shop. We ate, we laughed, we learned, we were stretched and filled with compassion. But there was a greater lesson, a harder lesson waiting for me and it came through an e-mail sent to my husband.

I was sitting cross-legged on a hilariously uncomfortable couch with my Bible and my heart open when KJ walked in. There was no drama, no fanfare, and no big hurrah. He is a man of few words and he said it simply.

"Ralph is dead. My parents sent me an e-mail this morning."

My captor, my grandfather, the one who had stolen 13 years of my life was finally dead. The one who had ravaged my body and my mind and still haunted my nightmares was gone. Vanished. Dead. Just like that, the enemy finally vanquished. It seems I should have felt relief but instead I was immediately overwhelmed with inexplicable grief. Tears sprang from my eyes as if leaping to their death, committing suicide on the open pages of my Bible. It was not that I cried, crying would be a woefully inadequate description. I ran to the bedroom and crumpled behind the closed door, I wept. I wept deep wrenching sobs. Open-throated visceral grief poured out. My heart was torn open and instead of relief I felt profound loss. For three days, the grief did not subside. I functioned on auto pilot. Tears constantly spent were replenishing themselves and pressing against the dam of my walled up heart until overwhelmed they flooded over into my days and nights. My husband did not understand, nor did I.

Late in the afternoon of the third day, he came in and seeing my red nose and tear-streaked face, his tender frustration had reached its limit.

"What is the deal?! He is dead!" he exclaimed. "We have waited for years for him to die. Why are you crying?"

Shaking my head, bewildered I choked out the only words that would come, "I don't know."

I could not grasp the reason behind my grief but I knew I had to figure it out. I returned to our bedroom and fell on my knees at the side of the bed. For three days I had cried but in that moment, I cried out to God. What follows is written just as I prayed it, one long, run-on, snot- dripping sentence.

"Jesus! I don't know why I am crying...I just hurt so bad...It hurts Jesus...It hurts because before he died I wanted to know that it mattered...somewhere deep inside of me I needed to know that all Ralph took from me...all that was stolen by force...the blood, the tears, the pain....that it was worth something...Jesus, I didn't expect an apology...I wouldn't have taken my kids back there for Christmas dinner...but I just needed to know that all it cost me was worth something...that it mattered...that I matter...now he is dead and I will never know..."

My sobs grew quiet and my tears fell mute and Jesus entered in. I did not see Him that afternoon in the slums of Peru but I heard His voice distinctly. It was loud, it was clear and it was unmistakably familiar.

"It mattered, Child. I wrote it down. Go read Judges 19," Jesus said simply.

A warm comfort descended and the peace became palpable. I grabbed my Bible and opened to the familiar and despised passage. I read it again with new eyes. I saw our little concubine sister the same way. I saw the cowardly priest saving his own skin. I saw men protected and the woman used and thrown away. I heard the door slam and the sounds of brutality, all the same way. The details of the story did not change. But through the ages the story has been preserved. It is recorded and guarded in the canon of scripture. Our little sister is not alone in her trauma. It was written down. Across the span of centuries we can enter in. We can sit with her and she can sit with us.

Here is what my trauma-blinded heart had not ever recognized. Her story is written down and memorialized in the Bible not because it is an endorsement of violence against women. It is not recorded there to justify exploitation and inequality. This story is written down only because every tiny detail mattered. God wrote it down because He, the creator of the universe, took note.

In the years prior to that day I had been too sickened by Judges 19 to continue reading. When I came to that story I would leave my Bible for days, sometimes weeks before my anger settled enough to return. But that afternoon at the side of the bed, I found an epilogue of sorts. Judges chapter 20 continues and finishes the story of our little sister and it finishes with brutal and bloody justice. The other 11 tribes of Israel formed an army to go arrest and execute the girl's murderers. When the local townspeople protected them instead, a war was ignited. By the end of the third day, only 600 men from the offending Benjamite tribe remained to bury their 25,000 dead brothers. There was justice for her.

My grandfather went to his grave with curses against God on his lips. He entered eternity with profanity and vile rejection of Him who is our Hope. Ralph will live out eternity enduring the wrath that his actions warranted. There is always justice.

And what of our little sister in Judges? She is not nameless. I think maybe, just maybe, we are not told her name for two reasons. First, because just as we do not report the name of minors who are sexually assaulted to protect them from further shame and exploitation, God is our first and best Defender. The second reason could be that she represents each one of us who have suffered senseless violence; the children who have died at the hands of wicked men; those who have faced the unimaginable, alone and afraid. My story is written into the shadows of hers. Perhaps yours is as well. It mattered, dear one. The Most High God took note. He wrote it down.

Right now, I invite you to stay here just awhile longer. Enter into our little sister's story in Judges 19 and 20, enter into mine. Better still, I invite you to enter fully into your own story. In this moment, take a deep breath square your shoulders and face bravely the scenes that have unfolded. You can do it. You are not alone. You have never really been alone.

What characters do you relate to? Have you been the object of pointless violence? Have you known the careless father or the wicked priest? Have you been cast out, vulnerable and unprotected? Dare I ask an even harder question? Have you been the one who sacrifices another to save your own skin?

Ultimately, we have all been on all sides of this equation in one degree or another. We all like sheep have gone astray. Where are your wounds? Where is your sin? Your story has not gone unnoticed, and it will not go unanswered. Do not make the mistake that I did, dear one, do not reject the One who has fought for your freedom for a moment longer. Justice is coming and the victory is sure.

CHAPTER 11

Give Me Liberty
or Give Me Death

I began my senior year in high school no longer holding out hope
for rescue. I believed that death offered my only escape. I had
longed for it for most of my life and could not wait any longer for
the gift of it to come. So like the child who sneaks into closets and
under beds in search of that hidden Christmas present, I sought out
death.

Starvation seemed to me a fairly reasonable and pain free way to
make the trip my heart longed for to the grave. So I began my journey by severely restricting what I would eat. By "severely restricting" I mean that I would not eat anything at all for 2 days, and then
on the third day I would allow myself to have one glass of chocolate
milk or one grilled cheese sandwich. That's it. The pounds that I did

not have to spare to begin with, began falling off of my body as I wasted away. I found that after about 2 weeks, it became fairly easy. It felt good to have control over one thing in my life and eventually I simply forgot to be hungry. Months passed as my 5'5" frame dropped slowly from 125 lbs. down to 120, 115, 105, 89 lbs. I was fainting regularly, at school and at work, my heart raced and I could hear my pulse echoing fast in my ears. My long, sandy blonde hair turned a dull, mousy brown and was falling out in handfuls. I knew that success loomed on the horizon and I rejoiced at the thought.

Then Ralph stepped in yet again. Rape. Degradation. Hopelessness. His power always loomed large and inescapable.

It was near the end of my senior year and my grandparents had invited us to vacation with them at their condo in Palm Springs, California over spring break. During that week the tectonic plates of my reality shifted. In the dark early hours of one morning, Ralph came into my bedroom and took what he had come for. Afterward, he sat on the side of the bed and laid out five crisp $100 bills on the nightstand. That money, rather than being payment for services rendered was a down payment on an unholy business contract. He smoothed the blankets and whispered tales of wealth and freedom.

"You are all grown up now. I just want you to know that if you would like to continue our arrangement then I will pay for your college... your own apartment... money... clothes... whatever you want, if only you will continue to make yourself available..." His voice was dark and soothingly lured me towards the abyss.

The thought of receiving money for something that had always been taken by force was ominously tempting. He had invested 13 years in training me to submit, and submit I had. But now the offer on the table forced me to consider becoming a willing participant and *only make myself available.* My body had been for sale since long before I had any grasp of the economics, but now it was my soul on the auction block. His new strategy offered me a strange power and suggested I was free to choose.

The right to say no had been scrubbed clean out of the fabric of my soul in a rose-colored bathtub years before. 'No' had not ever been a viable option and even now I knew it was not an option. Even so, in a bizarre twist, Ralph was offering the power to say 'yes.' The promise of money and provision shocked and drew me.

As a 17 year-old survivor, I had many questions and as you might imagine, a deeply distorted sense of personal value. Could it be that what I had to offer was worth something? Could I, personally, have any measurable worth? Over the years, I had come to believe that rescue was not ever coming. Maybe saying yes to this chance was as close to freedom as I would ever come. His words dripped honey sweetly poisonous.

A seismic shift was happening, and I was at the edge of myself, on the brink of destruction. Somehow I knew deep in my gut that if I said "yes" to Ralph not only would part of me die, but the most important part. Of all that he had taken from me, there remained one sacred, unreachable space within. That space, that fragment of a pure and unadulterated soul, was locked securely within the corridors of my imprisoned heart and it was the one thing that could not be reached by him, could not be taken by anyone without my consent. It would even take my husband 10 years of marriage to find this hidden key and free that piece of my heart.

Since "no" was not a word that any longer existed in my vocabulary and "yes" was seductive but impossible, I stumbled into a scalding shower and let the blistering water burn away the filth and the temptation. I emerged nearly an hour later with skin and heart blood red raw. I dressed and took the $500 cash to the nearest mall. In one afternoon of frivolous shopping, the money was spent in its entirety on gifts for my family. I came back to the condo and with a proud insolence I handed out the gifts. Then I turned to Ralph and dropped the change, all fifty-two cents worth, into his lap. I had spent $499.48 on my family and not one red cent on myself. My mouth could not form the word "no" so I screamed it as loudly as I could with my actions.

That day I concluded that my starvation plan was too slow of a course to take. As close as death seemed, it was still much too far away. I struggled for several weeks, starving, praying, and waiting stoically for it to come. But ultimately, I decided I would have to take more radical action.

One afternoon after school, I found a note from Ralph in my car. He had plans for me. Hysterical with grief I went home and ransacked the kitchen drawers in search of a knife. The time to act had come. I cut stripes in my left palm as I tested each blade. I wanted the sharpest knife I could find, because as bravely as I faced death, I genuinely dreaded more physical pain. I wrote a note to my parents and left it on my bed.

The cryptic goodbye read only this, "Don't open the bathroom door. Call the sheriff. I am sorry. There was just no other way."

I went into the bathroom around 4:30 in the afternoon and began filling the antique claw-foot tub with hot water. I reasoned that if I slit my wrists while in a hot bath I would bleed to death faster. With chest wracking sobs my soul howled of torment too long endured. My watery deathbed filled as I undressed.

And then, Jesus stepped in. I do not know how or even exactly when He stepped in this time. It is not out of shame or secrecy that I do not fill in the gap here but I truly have no recollection of the moments or hours that passed. Honestly, I do not know what happened next or exactly how God intervened into my wild grief.

Here is what I do remember. I woke up in the floor of the tiny bathroom with sharp knife still gripped tightly in my right hand.

Five small stripes had scabbed over on my left palm where I had sought out the best knife for my purpose. The bathtub was full to the brim of now cool water and I lay naked on top of the pile of clothes that I had discarded the afternoon before. I sat up slowly trying to orient myself. As I opened my blood-crusted right hand the joints ached and protested. My long, perfectly manicured fingernails left four deeply embedded half-moon cuts in my right palm from the steely grip I had held on the knife. But it was morning. It was time to get ready for school. I shook my head, trying to clear the fog. I was not dead and I had not been found. It was time for school. So, I did what all reasonable, straight A, high school seniors do. I tucked the knife into my makeup bag and got ready for school.

Most of that day passed like every other late spring day. It was April 26, 1990, two weeks before the senior prom and my 18th birthday. Final exams were looming and the excitement of graduation filled the air. But I walked the halls and attended classes as a ghost. Often throughout the day, my mind lingered on the Band-Aid covered stripes on my left hand and I wondered why I was still here. Why had I not succeeded?

After school that day I had an appointment at a Planned Parenthood clinic to receive information about methods of birth control. Little did I know at the time, but my plans for suicide were about to be undone by two little light blue lines. As storm clouds rolled across the horizon, I found out that I was pregnant. In an instant my entire existence shifted. Though abortion was offered as a possible solution, I knew that I could not, would not under any circumstances, be responsible for the death of an innocent child. Enough innocence had been lost.

I had been dating the same boy for two years by then and even though he and I were involved in a physical relationship he had no idea of the double life I was living. Adding mystery to trauma, there was no way for me to know for sure who the father of my child was. Even still, what I did know beyond a shadow of a doubt, was that this one sacred life was one that I would guard with everything I had. That meant that I would be forced to live instead of die. I would have to live at least long enough to give him life, long enough to see him safe and free. As much as I longed for death, it would have to be postponed because as long as an innocent child dwelt within me, suicide was not an option.

God sent a son to save my life-His perfect sinless one to extend me saving grace and my beautiful, imperfect one to buy me time. And more time was exactly what I needed. It would take a lot of it for me to begin to understand who God is and how He carries out His purposes, it would take even longer for me to begin to trust Him.

Unfortunately, the church offered no help at all for me. It should have been a place of grace, a safe haven embracing the broken. But as you may know, churches are made up of equally fallen people and we all have our own agendas. I had always suspected Brother Wayne was a good man if one truly existed, but he had since moved on, as had our family. My new pastor had a different view of the gospel than the one I heard and received when I was 14. Two weeks after I found out I was pregnant, I made an appointment to speak with him. I knew I needed to step down from my positions as a Sunday school teacher and youth leader and believed it was only appropriate to tell the pastor first. Instead of encountering someone Christlike that afternoon, I came face-to-face with the searing indignation of a Pharisee. He did not hold back either his disappointment or his judgment against my sin. He laid out his demands for penance precisely.

"You have two choices here. Either you will get up in front of the congregation on Sunday morning and confess your sin and you will ask them for their forgiveness or you will leave the church."

I answered him with an otherworldly poise and cool dignity, "I understand that I should not be a leader in the church anymore, but I will not confess to them and ask for their forgiveness. Not this. This is between me and God alone."

"No," he argued. "Sin impacts the whole church. You have a choice to make. Understand this, an unrepentant sinner will not be welcome here."

With his words the gavel slammed down on my stone-cold heart. A rebellion was sparked. I walked out of the church that afternoon with my shoulders back and head held high. I would not look back for nearly three years. I entered my freshman year of college six months pregnant and utterly alone. I registered at the small, liberal arts school as a double major in world religion and biology. If the God of the Bible was neither trustworthy nor true then I determined that it was time for me to figure out who or what was.

My firstborn tore his way into my world at 7:01 p.m. on December 13, 1990 on the first day of Christmas break. My labor was mercifully short. In a mere four hours and twenty-one minutes, I trekked the thousand mile distance from being a fragile woman-child to becoming a mother.

Completely unmedicated and utterly defiant, I cried out only once against the raging pain. Twelve minutes before he was born I shouted, "This is too much! I am too little for this. I am going home!" Those nearby chuckled at my futile threats.

And then suddenly there he was in my arms, this beautiful, bloody, blue-eyed mess of squawking life. A man-cub emerged from me and yet he was so mysteriously different from me. Despite my rejection of religion and my wandering soul, God in His mercy did not reject me and He would not let me go. Rather He showered me with grace upon grace. God had not only saved my life and given me more time but He used the birth of my son to awaken in me a mama bear instinct. I had never been able to take a stand and successfully defend myself but now there was an innocent child in the equation. For this little one, I knew I would stand and fight to the death. Rescue had finally come in a seven pound four ounce bundle. In his tiny tight fisted grip I found the strength to hold on and in his helpless wailing I finally found my voice.

I had lived in the shadowlands my entire life, but light was finally beginning to dawn. I named my son Grayson. It means to see more than black and white and it seemed only fitting. Somewhere between the black reality of the fallen world that I lived in and the white future that was promised there are the shadows, long and misty, obscuring the sun. The shadows of who I was and who I was meant to be; the cold shadows of a slow dying, the shadows of betrayal and of hope laid down, they all haunt the gray in between. Grayson was my son of the shadows and his birth gave life to him and me, both.

You may have found, as I did, that the church often fails those it is commissioned to help. It often can pose the single greatest obstacle to people finding and living out genuine faith and by contrast it is also one of the greatest evidences of the veracity of the gospel that has ever existed. The pastor on that spring day in 1990 tossed on the final straw that broke this little camel's back. I walked away.

I walked away from a judgmental preacher and from my grandfather who had been a respected leader in his church for years. I walked away from the child-rapists sitting innocuously on pews next to their plastic wives. I walked away from "How Great Thou Art" and from promises of deliverance that never seemed to materialize. I walked away from organized religion. I walked away from it all.

Whatever church was supposed to be, I had not found it. I knew that if what I had experienced in church was what the God of the Bible intended then I wanted nothing to do with it. Perhaps you too have been failed by the church.

Perhaps you have been betrayed by those who call themselves Christians. They gossip, they bite, and they manipulate, lie, cheat and steal. Occasionally they even rape. It is inexcusable and it is not as it was meant to be. Here is the thing though, we are all sinners, even those of us who call ourselves Christians. Our faith cannot hinge on wrecked humanity but instead the foundation of our faith must rest in Christ alone. If we are looking for our peace, our satisfaction, our joy in other people we are doomed to disappointment. People will fail us every time. But the Sinless One, the Perfect One who never leaves us nor forsakes us, will not ever fail us. It is so easy to itemize the sins against us; but it is so much harder to look in the mirror and see the truth of our own sinful reflection.

Have you ever been the one to gossip? Have you lied? Have you cheated? Perhaps you have taken what did not belong to you. I, for one, am guilty. I have been the prideful one who sits in judgment. I have been the manipulator, the liar and the thief. I have hated with murderous thoughts and ached for bloody vengeance. Perhaps your sins have been nicer than mine, perhaps a lighter shade of black, but make no mistake, we are all guilty to one degree or another. You and I, we stand together condemned, guilty as charged. That is exactly why the church is also one of the greatest evidences of the truth of the gospel. The fact that the church, made up of rascals, thieves and liars, exists more than 2,000 years after the death and resurrection of Jesus makes an undeniable argument.

The church was started by eleven broken men; sinful, impulsive, unrefined, chosen men. But they were men who had personally encountered Jesus and they had been changed by Him. The eleven chosen ones were cowards who went into hiding after Jesus' crucifixion. It was only after Jesus' resurrection on the third day that they came out and eventually became the men who would change the world. When they encountered Jesus, risen from the grave, their faith and passion could not and would not ever be restrained again. That faith eventually led ten of them to their martyrdom and one sentenced to life imprisoned in exile. But before their lives could be cut short the eleven became thousands, the thousands became millions and we today are their descendants.

Like our forefathers in the faith, we are each chips off the old block with our own selfish motives, cowardice and agendas. Therein lies the mystery and the miracle. The fact that the church not only still exists but that it moves forward when it is made up of broken, sinful people is a miracle of the same dramatic proportion as the parting of the Red Sea.

Miracles are still happening all around you every day. They happen when someone meets the living Jesus and is changed by Him, every time someone chooses to put their faith in the God that they cannot see, every time we repent and surrender ourselves to Him who is over all and through all and in all the gospel moves forward. Every time we choose love over hate, compassion over rejection, action over apathy; every time we nourish a starving soul or comfort a broken heart, every time we embrace those who are sinners just like us, we find ourselves embraced in return. The grace and the healing flows both ways. The one extending love receives no less than the one receiving it.

Please do not hear me justifying sinful behavior of a church or an individual. I am not justifying it, but rather telling the truth about it. The heinous acts that we have experienced at the hands of others are not okay. They are never justifiable. My grandfather should never have been allowed a position of authority and leadership in a church and a pastor who does not understand grace has no business in the pulpit. Whatever betrayal you have faced inside or outside of a church is neither justifiable nor excusable, but hang with me here-this is going to hurt a bit-neither is our own sin justifiable.

If this book is still in your hands and you have not thrown it out the window yet, stay with me one moment more, please? Get a piece of paper and lay out your charges against those who have sinned against you. Be specific in itemizing how those who should have helped you betrayed you instead. All that wrath and rage, pour it out with pen and ink.

Then, dear one, look in the mirror of your own heart. See yourself as the Righteous One sees you. Itemize your own sins and your own failures. Be they many or few, refuse the impulse to make excuses. Read the charges against your own soul and then lay them down before the Judge and raise your hands in surrender. Look into the face of the Resurrected One who died to pay your penalty. See His love for you and accept His mercy. Allow yourself to be changed by the One who calls you to be holy and blameless in His sight. He is still calling, "Come, follow me." Right now, you can choose to shake off the old and walk away from the past. You can choose to step into who Jesus made you to be.

As surely as you and I have failed others, the church will likely fail us in any number of ways. But Jesus, He is our source of faith and His grace is enough. Jesus is, even now, weaving each of us into one body, the beautiful, still imperfect church. It is there in community and in fellowship that our gifts, our skills and our assets make up for all of our collective inadequacies. It is a place where a thousand fragments of love throbbing in broken hearts can come together as one whole. It is there that His light can become a beacon shining into the darkness through all of our broken places.

You were made for more, dear one. You were made for glory and to do good works which He prepared in advance for you. Take a deep breath and jump with both feet into the life He has for you.

Epilogue

- The horrific realities of Jenni's childhood were later independently documented by the Menninger Clinic of Topeka, Kansas. Clinical evidence and psychological examinations obtained indicate that her accounts were neither exaggerated nor minimized.

- The unsolved case of the man killed in the hit and run accident was tracked down by a private investigator and later confirmed by the Missouri State Police.

- Unfortunately, the statute of limitations expired before Jenni was able to present her case in criminal court. Ralph died cursing God with his very last breath.

- Three other survivors have come forward and disclosed similar stories of the trauma they endured at Ralph's hand. In an effort to protect their identities and honor their autonomy no reference has been made to them in this book.

- Jenni met KJ, the love of her life, in January 1993 and has now been in love with him for more than half of her life. Shortly after they married in 1994, KJ adopted Jenni's son Grayson.

- Due to the extensive damage done during her childhood, Jenni has suffered several miscarriages. She and her husband went on to conceive and carry 15 more beloved babies; 13 of whom died in utero and were born directly into glory. They thank God everyday for the miracles of Scarlet and Maverek, born in 1997 and 1999 respectively.

- Grayson, Scarlet, and Maverek were home-schooled by Jenni while KJ led their family in pursuing a missional lifestyle. Together they have lived and served in 4 US states and in 3 countries.

- The Jessen family now resides and works in SE Asia where they founded Compass 31. They have dedicated their lives to making Jesus known by fighting human trafficking through prevention, restoration and disciple making. (www.compass31.org)

- KJ and Jenni were able to use their experience in the anti-human trafficking field to create Priceless Cube, a tool designed to prevent human trafficking through education. It is currently in use in more than 40 countries. (www.pricelesscube.com)

- Additionally, by providing foster care to a tribe of teenage mothers and babies rescued from the sex trade, the Jessen family has the privilege of watching redemption come full circle again and again. It is a crazy-beautiful life.

It is our deepest desire that God would be glorified in all and through all. If this book has touched you, you can correspond with Jenni and her family by writing to: theluckyone@compass31.org

Compass 31

Compass 31 exists to make Jesus known by fighting human trafficking through prevention, restoration, and disciple making.

- **Prevention:** Compass 31 uses Priceless Cube to prevent human trafficking through education. In partnership with e3 Partners, this tool is being successfully implemented in high risk areas of exploitation in more than 40 countries. www.pricelesscube.com

- **Restoration:** Compass 31 provides family-based foster care to teenage survivors of sex trafficking who are pregnant or have babies as a result of their exploitation. Our Christ centered model includes assisting the survivors in finding freedom, mentally, physically and spiritually. The survivors are empowered to gain an education and pursue a safe and better future while being supported with art and music therapy, small groups, language lessons, childcare and even classes in financial planning and management.

- **Disciple Making:** Compass 31 trains nationals to share the transformative gospel of Jesus Christ in culturally relevant ways. Those leaders are then equipped to be the first line of defense, protecting the vulnerable in their own communities from exploitation.

At Compass 31 we believe that God uses ordinary people to make an extraordinary difference. You can join us in the fight and have a significant impact in three following ways.

1. **Pray** – Jesus is the only solution to the worldwide epidemic of slavery and prayer is our most vital resource and critical need. The prayers of a righteous man avail much. By signing up to receive weekly prayer updates, you can join an army of warriors fighting to set captives free from their knees. In doing so, you will have the privilege of watching the dramas, victories, losses and miracles of our work at Compass 31 unfold in real time.
   To sign up: www.compass31.org/pray

2. **Give** – Compass 31 is a non-profit 501c3. The proceeds from the sale of this book will go, in their entirety, to the restoration of survivors. All projects and programs of Compass 31 are faith based and funded by tax deductible donations. The battle against human trafficking is not only long and hard but it is costly as well. Our fundraising paradigm is based on the fact that every 26 seconds a child is sold into slavery. We, at Compass 31, don't run from the fight. You are invited to participate in our "No Run Marathon" by committing to give $26 or more a month.
   To give: www.compass31.org/give

3. **Raise Awareness** – Human trafficking has been documented in every country in the world and every U.S. state. The average age of entry into the U.S. sex trade is 11 years old; globally that average age drops to 9 years old. A child has a life expectancy of 7 years or less once they have been taken into captivity. You can have an impact by arming yourself with PricelessCube. Use your growing knowledge and passion for justice to prevent human trafficking through education your own community and in the farthest reaches of the globe.
   To learn more: www.pricelesscube.com

Additional Resources

Understanding Human Trafficking:

- "Nefarious: Merchant of Souls | A Documentary on the Global Sex Trade." Nefarious Documentary Trilogy. Web. 28 Mar. 2016. www.nefariousdocumentary.com by Exodus Cry.

Finding Personal Healing and Restoration:

- Allender, Dan B. The Wounded Heart Hope for Adult Victims of Childhood Sexual Abuse. Colorado Springs, CO: NavPress, 1990. Print.

- Allender, Dan B., and Tremper Longman. Bold Love. Colorado Springs, CO: NavPress, 1992. Print.

- Mending the Soul Ministries – www.mendingthesoul.com

Best Practices and Restoration Models for Survivors:

- Tracy, Celestia G., Kayla L. Tracy, George MacDonald, George MacDonald, and George MacDonald. *Princess Lost: The Story of Our Daughters.* Phoenix, AZ: Mending the Soul, 2011. Print.

- Tracy, Steven R., Celestia G. Tracy, and Celestia G. Tracy. *Princess Found: A Guide for Mentors of Sexually Exploited Girls.* Phoenix, AZ: Mending the Soul, 2011. Print.

Made in the USA
San Bernardino, CA
24 February 2017